QUILTS FROM
paradise

Cynthia Tomaszewski

Martingale®
& COMPANY

DEDICATION

For my son, Zachary, the other great love of my life. You've grown from a small boy to a young man of whom I am so very proud. You are wise beyond your years. I wish only good things for you, but above all else, I wish you happiness, love, laughter, and contentment. If you have these, you will find your place in the sun, your personal paradise, wherever life takes you.

Quilts from Paradise
© 2009 by Cynthia Tomaszewski

That Patchwork Place® is an imprint of Martingale & Company®.

Martingale & Company
20205 144th Ave. NE
Woodinville, WA 98072-8478 USA
www.martingale-pub.com

Printed in China
14 13 12 11 10 09 8 7 6 5 4 3 2 1

Library of Congress Cataloging-in-Publication Data
Library of Congress Control Number: 2009017936

ISBN: 978-1-56477-902-1

mission statement

Dedicated to providing quality products and service to inspire creativity.

credits

President & CEO: Tom Wierzbicki
Editor in Chief: Mary V. Green
Managing Editor: Tina Cook
Developmental Editor: Karen Costello Soltys
Technical Editor: Ellen Pahl
Copy Editor: Marcy Heffernan
Design Director: Stan Green
Production Manager: Regina Girard
Illustrator: Laurel Strand
Cover & Text Designer: Shelly Garrison
Photographer: Brent Kane

CONTENTS

PREFACE

Paradise is really the journey. It's not a place. It's not your destination. It's in the love, the laughter, the happiness, those moments of pure joy we experience along the way. It's in the hopes, the dreams, the fantasies, the plans, the details, and the construction. It's the teaming with someone who shares your dreams and the journey. It's the special moments that happen in our lives.

I think we all question the humdrum routine of our existence—the obligations and the commitments, schedules, endless bureaucracy, and gadget overload that tend to push us to the limit. We dream of escape.

But I think Paradise is about finding your rhythm, about making time for the things you absolutely love and treasure, and for the special people who are important to you. It's having a sense of purpose and appreciation. It's about saying "yes" and saying "no" and having the wisdom to know when to use the correct one. Everything in life is a choice. You choose. That's reality. So choose wisely. Sometimes we need to say no so we have time to say yes to Paradise.

I have a 3-ring binder. It's nothing fancy, but it contains notes from what I call the really great books that I have read—those books that inspire me to look at the world through fresh eyes. The notes I've saved are my wake-up calls. They remind me to restrain myself and only say yes to the important things. I keep the binder on the shelf in my studio and page through it regularly, particularly when I'm feeling stressed and hassled, and then I always realize that I haven't taken the time to visit Paradise.

My favorite page in my 3-ring binder is "My Life List." I started it years ago, and I update it at times. In the left column is "The Things I Love," and in the right column is "My Fantasy List." I'm a real believer in lists. I believe if you dream it, you write it down, it will happen.

"My Fantasy List" is what gives me that sense of purpose and gratitude. It's what I'm working on. It's my list, so I can put whatever I want on it; things like, have my own business, design my perfect house, learn to paint, live in an exotic culture, walk the Great Wall of China, have a garden, learn ballet, share my love of quilting, get a Jeep. I can add big things or small things. They are things I believe will make me happy, grow and expand, give me an opportunity to interact with others, and keep my sense of adventure alive.

It's my "The Things I Love" list that is my Paradise list. I fill my vacation days doing the things I love, but if I can make time to do even just one or two things on my list every day, then I feel like I have gotten my piece of Paradise. Things like, listen to music, read, take a walk on the beach, chat with my son, arrange some flowers, go fishing, have a coffee and people watch, browse in a bookstore, have a candlelight bath, visit a gallery, watch the sun rise or set, write a letter to my friend, bake, quilt, make love in the afternoon, see a good movie, have dinner in an ethnic restaurant, meet with a friend, run—they are the rewards that I give myself. They make me feel happy, and when I'm happy I want to make everyone around me happy. These things make me appreciate life and all the crazy moments that make up the day. And if I never live to reach my ideal Paradise, it's okay because I have experienced a little of the best every day. Isn't that what life is all about?

I love this poem, and I wanted to share it with you. It says it best....

ITHACA

When you set out on your journey to Ithaca,
pray that the road is long,
full of adventure, full of knowledge.
The Lestrygonians and the Cyclops,
the angry Poseidon—do not fear them
You will never find such as those on your path
if your thoughts remain lofty, if a fine
emotion touches your spirit and your body.
The Lestrygonians and the Cyclops,
the fierce Poseidon you will never encounter,
if you do not carry them within your soul,
if your heart does not set them up before you.

Pray that the road is long.
That the summer mornings are many, when,
with such pleasure, with such joy
you will enter ports seen for the first time;
stop at Phoenician markets,
and purchase fine merchandise,
mother-of-pearl and coral, amber and ebony,
and sensual perfumes of all kinds,
as many sensual perfumes as you can;
visit many Egyptian cities,
to learn and learn from scholars.

Always keep Ithaca in your mind.
To arrive there is your ultimate goal.
But do not hurry the voyage at all.
It is better to let it last for many years;
and to anchor at the island when you are old,
rich with all that you have gained on the way,
not expecting that Ithaca will offer you riches.
Ithaca has given you the beautiful voyage.
Without her you would never have set out on the road.
She has nothing more to give you.

And if you find her poor, Ithaca has not deceived you.
Wise as you have become, with so much experience,
you must already have understood what Ithacas mean.

Constantine Cavafy (1863–1933)
Translated by Rae Dalven

I wish you a piece of Paradise every day. ~ Cynthia

INTRODUCTION

If you could escape to a paradise, just for you, today, right this minute, what would it be? Where would it be? What would it look like? It would be your haven, your place of total happiness and perfect beauty.

For me, it would be an island in a vast blue sea, surrounded by reefs and water a million shades of blue; brilliant sunlight glistening on the water…perfect white sand beaches littered only with shells, the sea's special gift for me; tall palms, fronds gently swaying in the breeze…colorful birds singing, fish jumping and playing in the waves; bright tropical flowers abounding; and jasmine and frangipani scenting the breeze. My hammock is at the water's edge, a fresh fruit drink cools my thirst…waves gently lap the shore…no thoughts trouble my mind. No worries. No demands. No schedules. I have time to just contemplate, to soul search…long lazy days to pamper myself, to indulge the senses, to experience nature…my mind and body at peace. Ahhh…Paradise!

Whether it's Asia or the islands of the Caribbean or the Pacific, they all possess a special magic that can only be found on the islands of the world. This sense of magic inspires creativity. Gauguin voyaged to Tahiti to find his special place. Anne Morrow Lindbergh's personal interlude to the seashore inspired her insights that she shares with us in *A Gift from the Sea*. Henri Matisse, James Michener, Herman Melville, Robert Louis Stevenson, and Ernest Hemingway all found inspiration in the magic of the islands.

Though we may not be able to spend our days languishing on the shores of a tropical paradise, we can still be inspired by their magic to create quilts of beauty that are instilled with the essence of the islands.

If your picture of paradise is something like mine, you will enjoy these designs filled with the spirit of the islands. They will embrace you with the feel of the sun, sea, and tropical breezes. They will touch you with the life force of the islands. Surrender yourself to the enchantment of a tropical isle.

~ *Cynthia*

ENTANGLED

Love, like the vines, clings and grows,
binding the hearts of special souls.

MATERIALS

Yardage is based on 42"-wide fabric.

1⅛ yards of light green batik for vines and leaves

⅝ yard of deep pink batik for large and medium hearts

½ yard each of 12 different multicolored medium to dark batiks for blocks and border

½ yard of batik for blocks and binding

¼ yard each of 2 different deep pink batiks for small hearts

3 yards of fabric for backing

52" x 67" piece of batting

3 yards of coordinating ¼" hand-dyed trim for border embellishment (optional)

CUTTING

All measurements include ¼" seam allowances. Save the scraps of the 13 batiks to use in the Crazy Patch blocks. Refer to "Appliquéing the Blocks" on page 10 before cutting the appliqué pieces.

From the 12 different multicolored batiks, cut:

6 of patch 1 using the template pattern on page 12

6½"-wide strips of various lengths for outer border to total approximately 210"

From the batik for blocks and binding, cut:

6 strips, 2" x 42"

From the deep pink batik for large and medium hearts, cut:

6 of template 1

6 of template 3

From the 2 deep pink batiks for small hearts, cut:

6 of template 2

6 of template 4

From the light green batik, cut:

½"-wide bias strips to total 222"

66 of template 5

24 of template 6

6 of template 6 reversed

Quilt size: 42" x 57" ❁ Block size: 15" x 15"

ASSEMBLING THE BLOCKS

Assemble the six center blocks using the crazy piecing technique. You will begin with patch 1 and add pieces using scraps from the 13 batik fabrics.

1. Begin each block with patch 1, right side up.

2. For patch 2, choose a scrap of batik fabric larger than patch 1 or cut a four-sided piece of fabric at least as big as patch 1. Lay it right side down on top of patch 1, lining up the raw edges along one side. Stitch ¼" from the raw edges.

3. Turn patch 2 right side up and press. Use scissors or a rotary cutter and ruler to trim patch 2; use the edges of patch 1 to make a straight-line cut on both sides of patch 2.

4. Cut a patch 3 and sew it to patches 1 and 2 in the same manner; turn, press, and trim. You can work in a counterclockwise or clockwise direction.

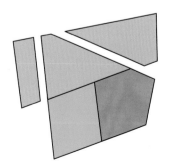

5. Continue adding patches around the pieced unit. Try to keep the sides from getting too long before adding the next patch. If any particular seam becomes too long, cut the pieced unit at an angle that will create a new side to attach a patch in such a way as to keep the building process going. Add patches until you have constructed a piece of fabric large enough from which to cut a 15½" square.

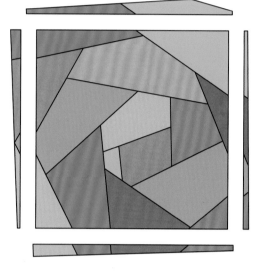

APPLIQUÉING THE BLOCKS

1. Choose your favorite appliqué method and make appliqué templates for the hearts and leaves by tracing the patterns on pages 12 and 13. Refer to "Introduction to Appliqué" on page 119 for details as needed.

2. Appliqué the four hearts to each of the six Crazy Patch blocks referring to the placement diagram on page 11 as needed.

3. Refer to "Making Bias Stems and Vines" on page 123 to make ¼"-wide bias strips from the green batik ½"-wide bias strips.

4. Appliqué the vines and leaves in position, referring to the placement diagram below.

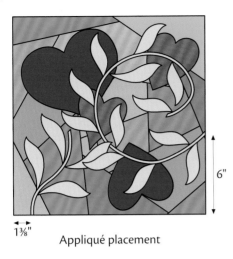

6"

1⅜"

Appliqué placement

ASSEMBLING THE QUILT

1. Assemble the quilt center by sewing three horizontal rows of two blocks each. Rotate the blocks so the design in each block faces in different directions. Refer to the quilt photo on page 9 for placement. Press the seam allowances in opposite directions from row to row. Sew the rows together.

2. To complete the borders, cut the ends of the 6½"-wide batik strips of various lengths at a 45° angle and sew them together. You will need two strips 6½" x approximately 36" and two strips 6½" x approximately 61". Try to have the same-color fabric at the strip ends where the corners will meet. When piecing the strips together, offset the seams ¼" as shown. Refer to the quilt photo on page 9 for placement.

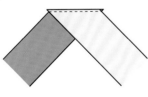

3. Optional: Sew coordinating hand-dyed trim on top of each 45°-angle seam line.

4. To add the top and bottom borders, measure across the center of your quilt. Trim both strips to this measurement and sew them to the top and bottom of the quilt center. Press the seam allowances toward the border strips.

5. To add the side borders, measure lengthwise through the center of the quilt, including the top and bottom borders. Trim the side borders to this measurement and sew them to the sides; press.

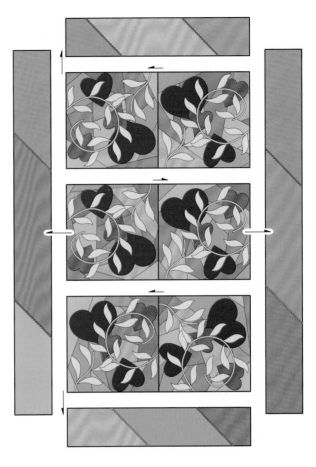

FINISHING THE QUILT

Refer to "Quiltmaking Basics" on page 111 for more details if needed.

1. Mark the quilting design on the quilt top if desired. See the quilting suggestion on page 13.

2. Layer the quilt top with batting and backing; baste or pin.

3. Quilt by hand or by machine.

4. Use the 2" x 42" batik strips to bind the edges of the quilt.

5. Add a label to the back of your quilt.

5
Cut 66.

3
Cut 6.

6
Cut 24 and 6 reversed.

Patch 1

2
Cut 6.

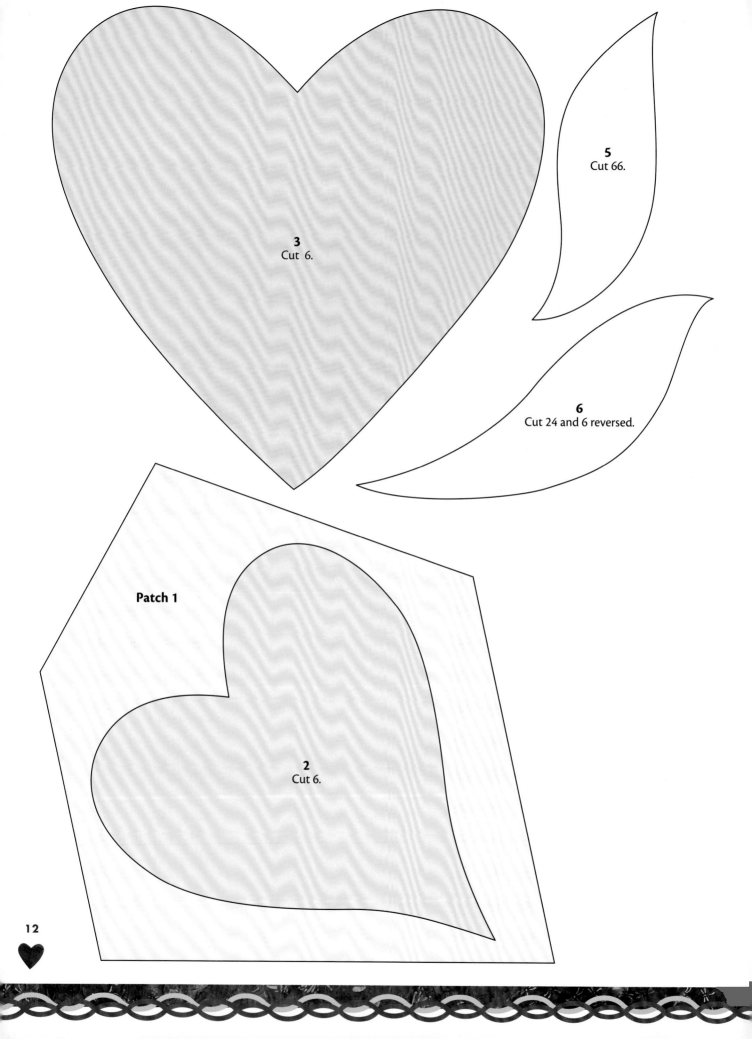

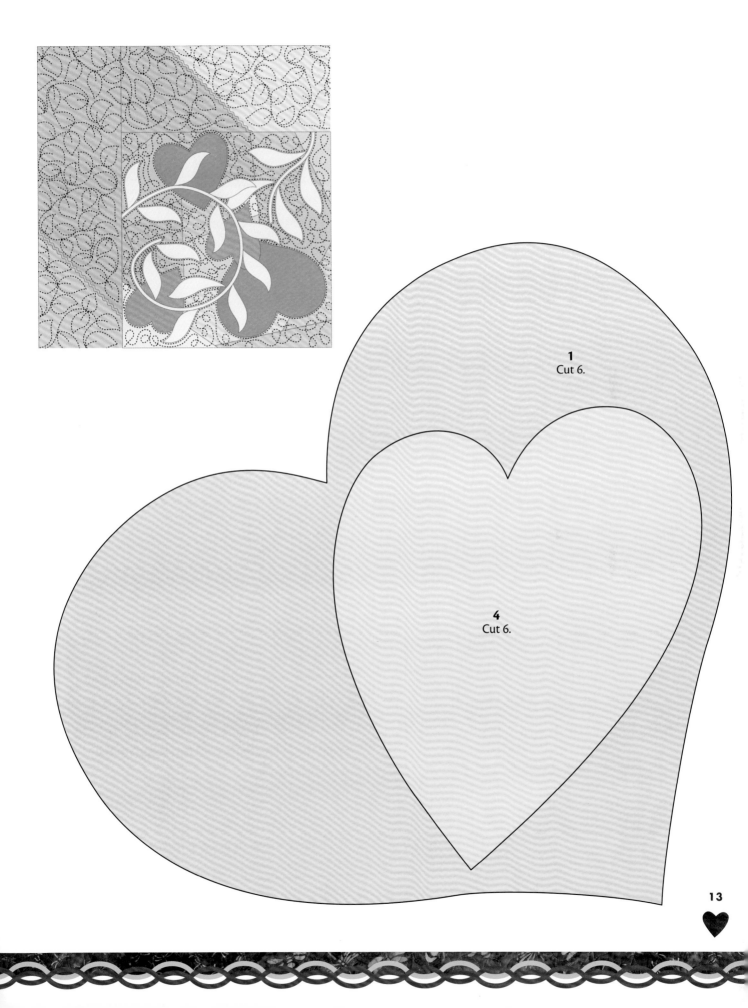

1
Cut 6.

4
Cut 6.

TROPICAL WHIMSY

Exotic flowers abound in the islands.
This fabulous quilt includes many of them in their wonderful, bright colors.

MATERIALS

Yardage is based on 42"-wide fabric.

2⅛ yards of yellow polka-dot fabric for border

1 yard of yellow-and-white striped fabric for blocks

½ yard of green print for bias stems, flowers, and leaves

⅓ yard each of 6 different green prints for flowers and leaves

26 fat quarters of bright fabrics for flowers, sashing, and optional binding*

¼ yard of yellow print for sashing squares

½ yard of fabric for binding (or use leftover scraps of bright fat quarters)

3½ yards of fabric for backing

60" x 78" piece of batting

*You can use fewer fat quarters if you don't mind repeating the fabrics in the sashing and appliqués.

CUTTING

All measurements include ¼"-wide seam allowances.

From the yellow-and-white striped fabric, cut:
12 rectangles, 8½" x 10½"

From the yellow print, cut:
20 squares, 2½" x 2½"

From the 26 fat quarters of bright fabrics, cut:
15 strips, 2½" x 8½"
16 strips, 2½" x 10½"

From the yellow polka-dot fabric, cut on the *lengthwise* grain:
2 strips, 9½" x 34"
2 strips, 9½" x 72"

From the binding fabric or leftover scraps of bright fat quarters, cut:
7 strips, 2" x 42" or cut 2"-wide strips to total 254"

Quilt size: 50" x 68" ❀ Block size: 8" x 10"

APPLIQUÉ CUTTING KEY

Refer to "Assembling the Quilt" (steps 1 and 3) below before cutting the appliqué pieces.

From the ½ yard of green print, cut:
½"-wide bias strips to total 90"

From the 26 fat quarters of bright fabrics, cut:
1 *each* of templates 1, 5–9, 16, 18, 19, 22, 23, 39–43, 48–52, 56–58, 62–67, 73, 75, 76, and 83–95

1 of template 25 and 1 of template 25 reversed

3 *each* of templates 30 and 32

5 of template 74

From the 6 different green prints for flowers and leaves and the remainder of the ½ yard of green print, cut:
1 *each* of templates 2–4, 11–15, 17, 20, 21, 24, 26–28, 34–38, 44–46, 53–55, 59–61, 68–72, 78, 79, 81, and 82

4 of template 10

7 of template 29

18 of template 31

3 of template 33

1 of template 47 and 1 of template 47 reversed

2 of template 77

2 of template 80

15 of template 96 and 15 of template 96 reversed

ASSEMBLING THE QUILT

1. Refer to "Making Bias Stems and Vines" on page 123 to make ¼"-wide bias strips from the green ½"-wide bias strips.

2. Appliqué the stems and vines in position on the yellow-and-white striped 8½" x 10½" rectangles. Refer to the pattern diagrams on pages 18–30 for placement guidance. Note that several of the leaves will need to be inserted underneath the stems. Leave openings for the leaves or proceed to steps 3 and 4 to add the leaves as you stitch the stems.

3. Choose your favorite appliqué method and make templates for the flowers and leaves by tracing the patterns on pages 18–30. Refer to "Introduction to Appliqué" on page 119 for details as needed. Cut out the number of each shape indicated in the "Appliqué Cutting Key."

4. Appliqué all leaves and flowers in position, referring to the photo on page 15 and the pattern diagrams for placement guidance.

5. Any thin vines or stems may be done using a stem stitch and two strands of 6-strand embroidery floss. Refer to "Embroidery Stitches" on page 120.

6. Sew five sashing rows consisting of four yellow 2½" sashing squares and three bright 2½" x 8½" sashing strips. Press toward the darker fabrics when possible.

Make 5.

7. Sew four rows consisting of three appliqué blocks and four bright 2½" x 10½" sashing strips; press.

Make 4.

8. Sew the rows together, alternating sashing and block rows to form the quilt center.

9. To add the top and bottom borders, measure across the center of your quilt. Trim the yellow polka-dot 9½" x 34" strips to this measurement and sew them to the top and bottom of the quilt center. Press the seam allowances toward the darker fabrics.

10. To add the side borders, measure lengthwise through the center of the quilt, including the top and bottom borders. Trim the side borders to this measurement and sew them to the sides of the quilt; press.

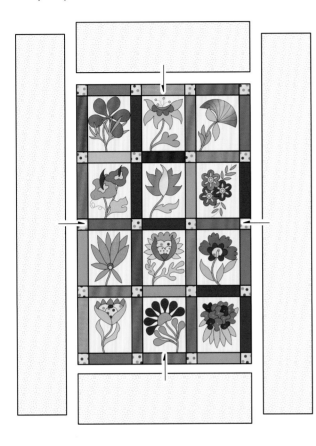

11. Appliqué 30 leaves to the border. Refer to the quilt photograph on page 15 for placement guidance.

FINISHING THE QUILT

Refer to "Quiltmaking Basics" on page 111 for more details if needed.

1. Mark the quilting design on the quilt top if desired. See the quilting suggestion below.

2. Layer the quilt top with batting and backing; baste or pin.

3. Quilt by hand or by machine.

4. Use the 2" x 42" strips or the miscellaneous 2" strips to bind the edges of the quilt.

5. Add a label to the back of your quilt.

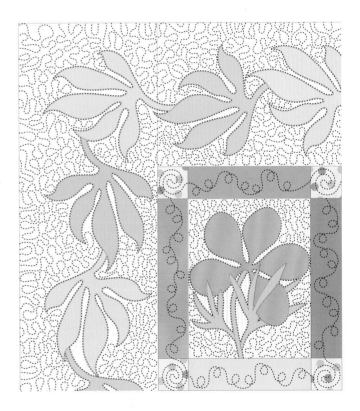

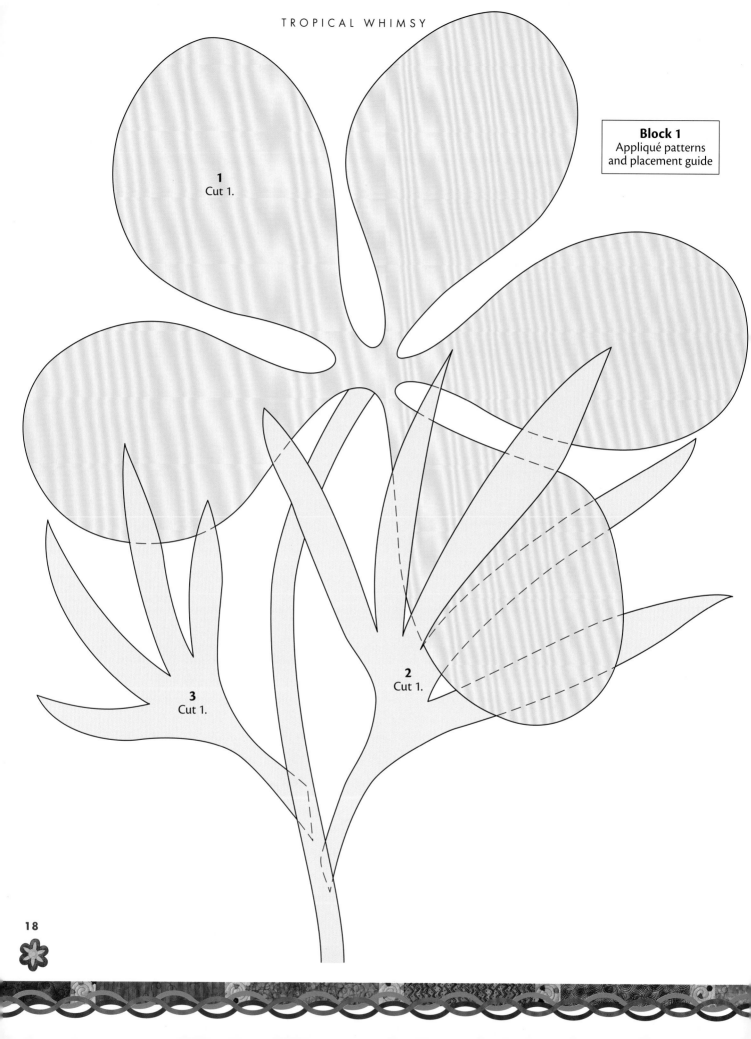

Block 1
Appliqué patterns
and placement guide

1
Cut 1.

2
Cut 1.

3
Cut 1.

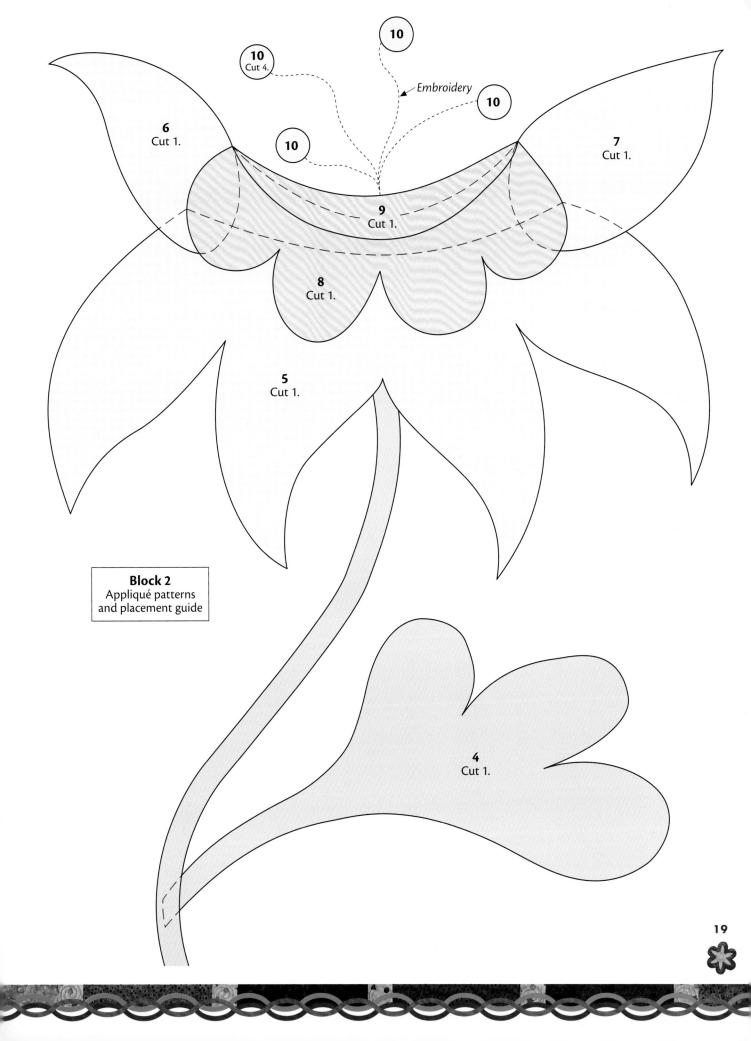

10

10
Cut 4.

10

← *Embroidery*

10

6
Cut 1.

7
Cut 1.

10

9
Cut 1.

8
Cut 1.

5
Cut 1.

Block 2
Appliqué patterns
and placement guide

4
Cut 1.

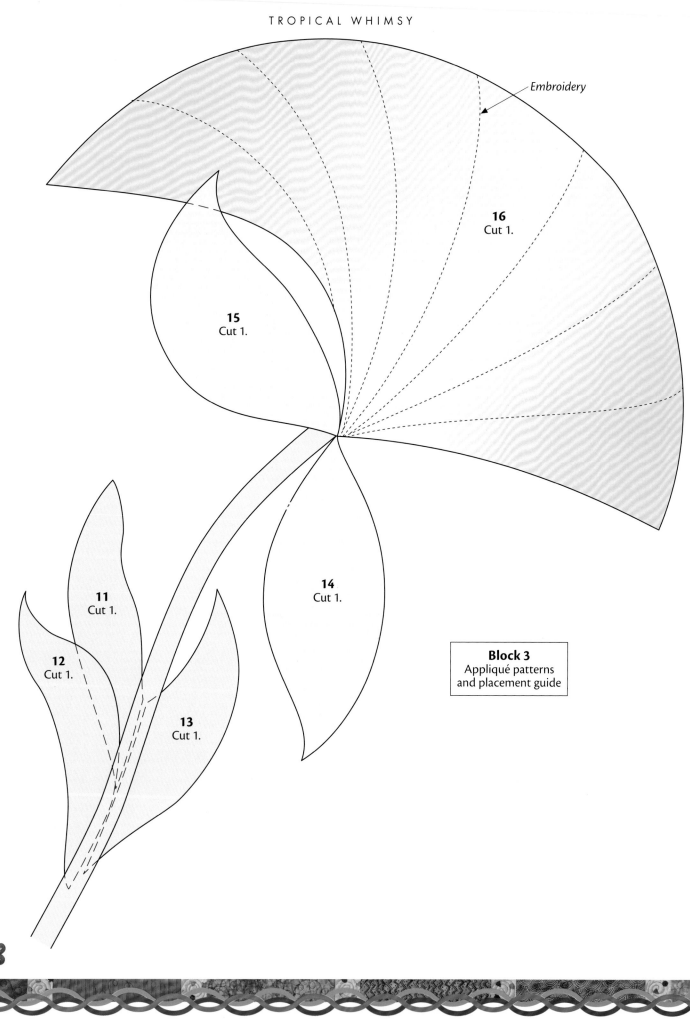

Embroidery

16
Cut 1.

15
Cut 1.

14
Cut 1.

11
Cut 1.

12
Cut 1.

13
Cut 1.

Block 3
Appliqué patterns
and placement guide

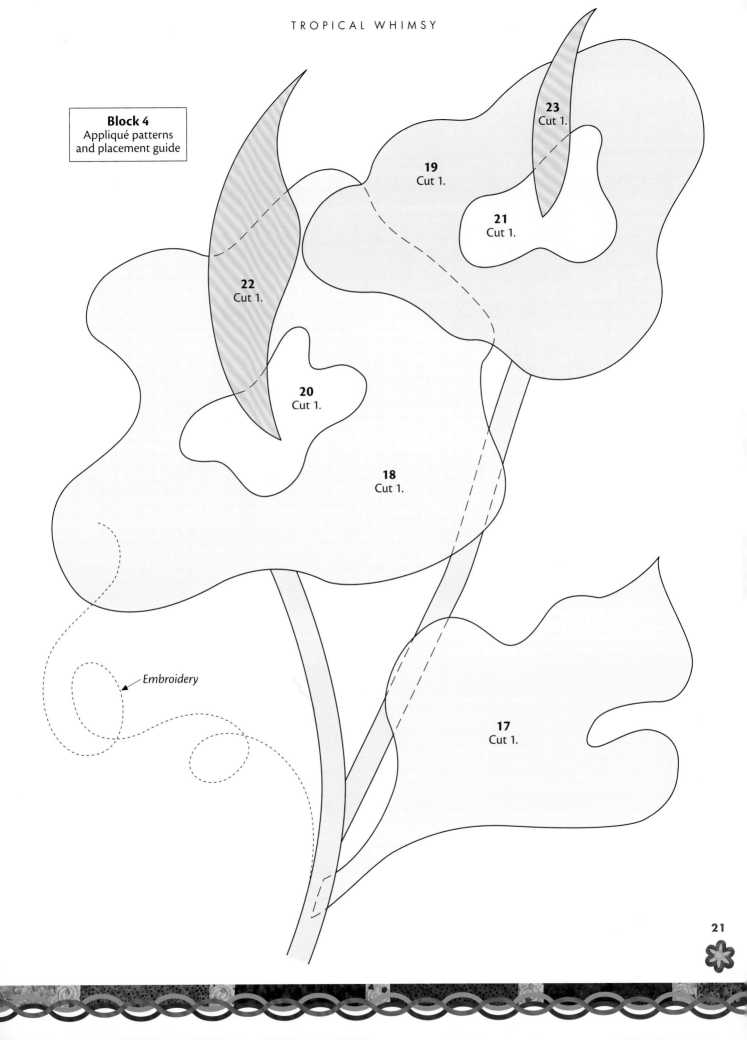

Block 4
Appliqué patterns
and placement guide

23
Cut 1.

19
Cut 1.

21
Cut 1.

22
Cut 1.

20
Cut 1.

18
Cut 1.

Embroidery

17
Cut 1.

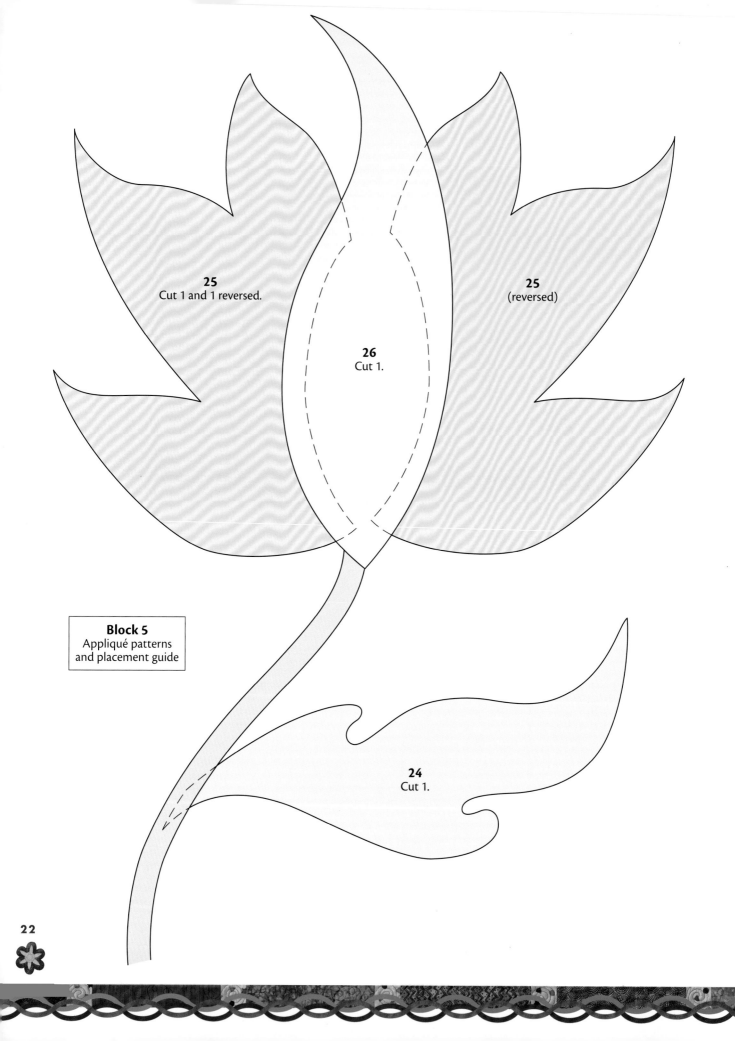

25
Cut 1 and 1 reversed.

25
(reversed)

26
Cut 1.

Block 5
Appliqué patterns
and placement guide

24
Cut 1.

Block 6
Appliqué patterns
and placement guide

Embroidery

27
Cut 1.

29
Cut 7.

28
Cut 1.

29

31

30
Cut 3.

31
Cut 18.

32
Cut 3.

31

33
Cut 3.

31

29

29

31

31

31

30

31

31

32

31

33

31

31

31

31

30

32

31

31

33

31

31

31

31

29

29

29

29

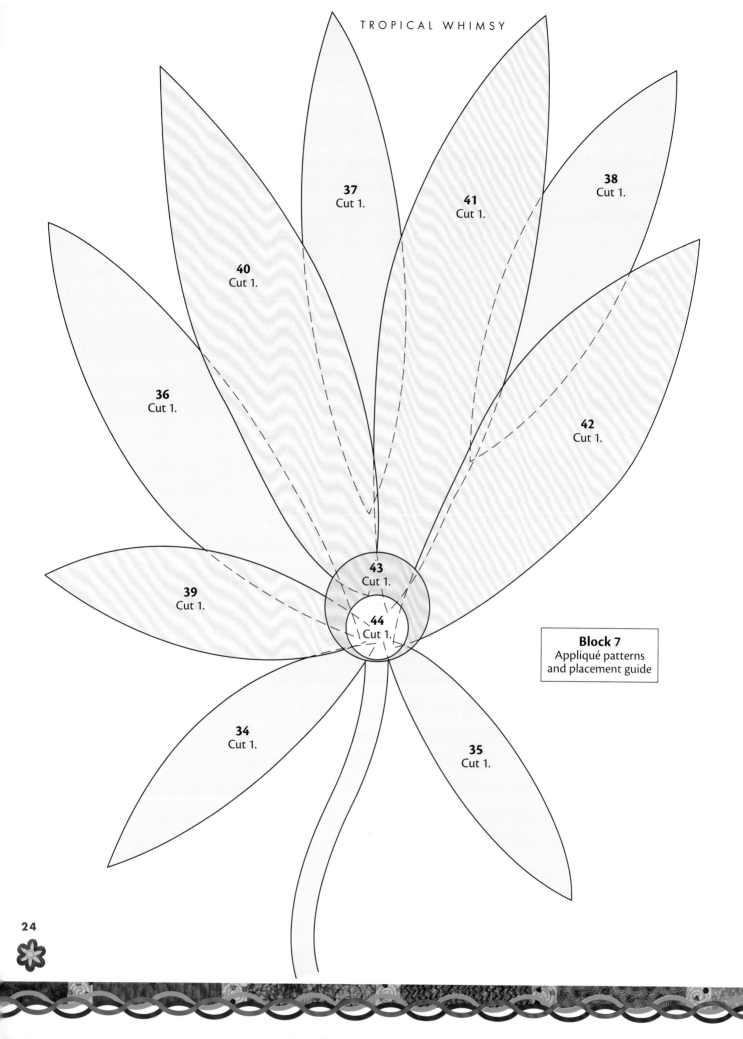

37
Cut 1.

41
Cut 1.

38
Cut 1.

40
Cut 1.

36
Cut 1.

42
Cut 1.

43
Cut 1.

39
Cut 1.

44
Cut 1.

Block 7
Appliqué patterns
and placement guide

34
Cut 1.

35
Cut 1.

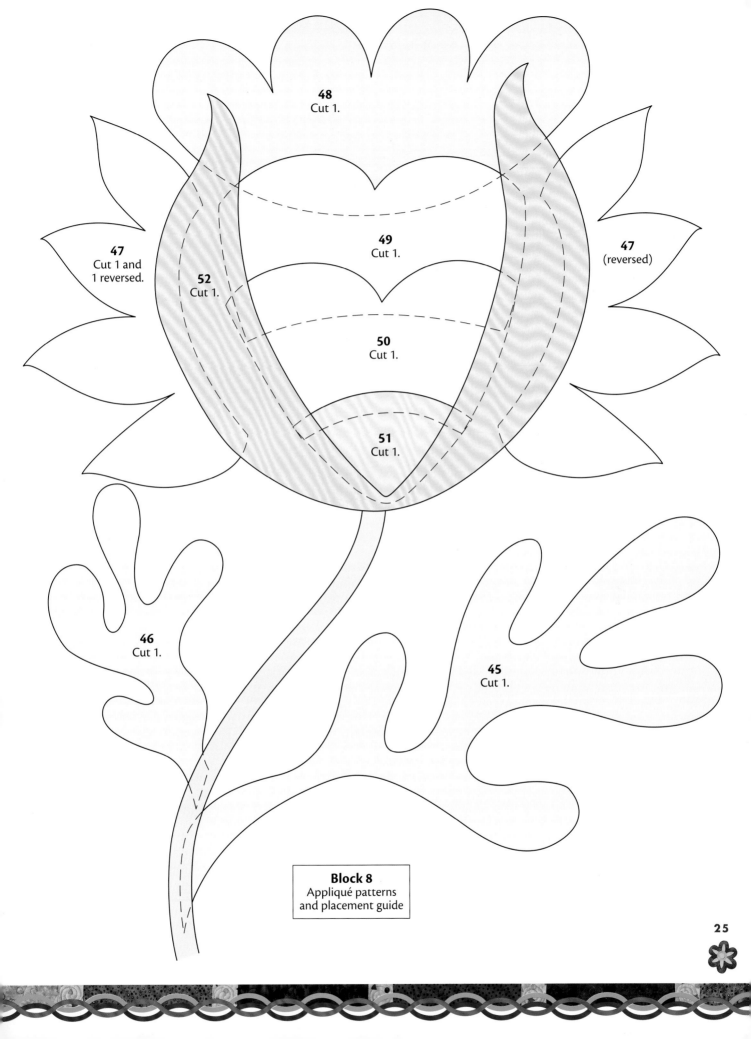

48
Cut 1.

47
Cut 1 and
1 reversed.

49
Cut 1.

52
Cut 1.

47
(reversed)

50
Cut 1.

51
Cut 1.

46
Cut 1.

45
Cut 1.

Block 8
Appliqué patterns
and placement guide

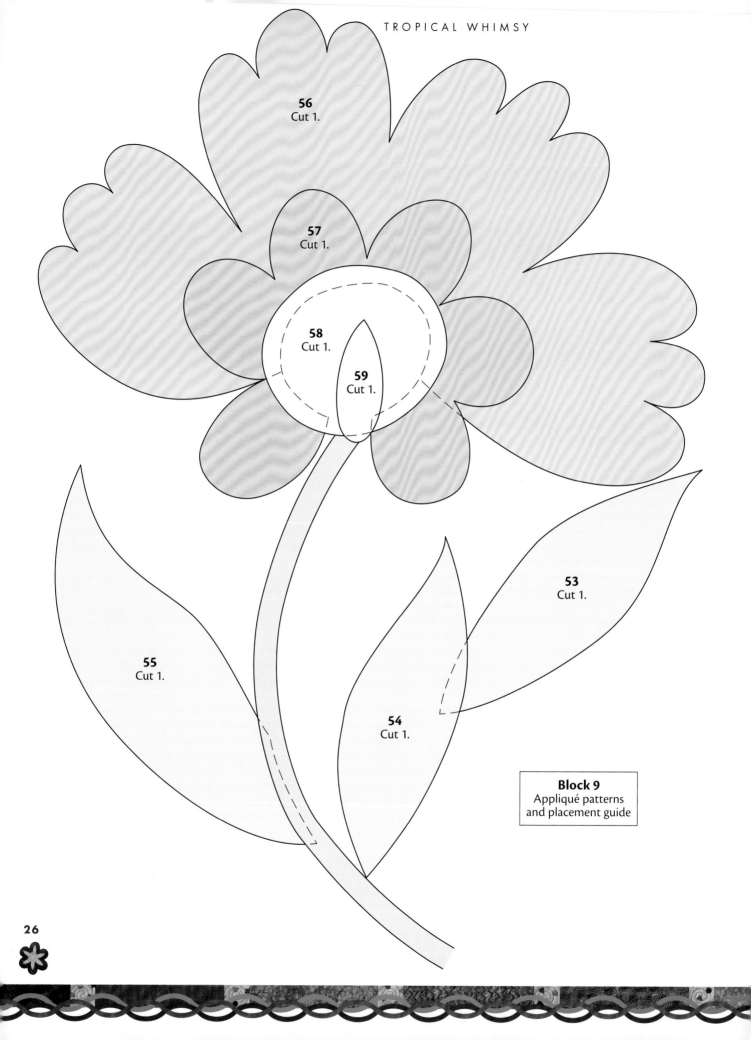

56
Cut 1.

57
Cut 1.

58
Cut 1.

59
Cut 1.

53
Cut 1.

55
Cut 1.

54
Cut 1.

Block 9
Appliqué patterns
and placement guide

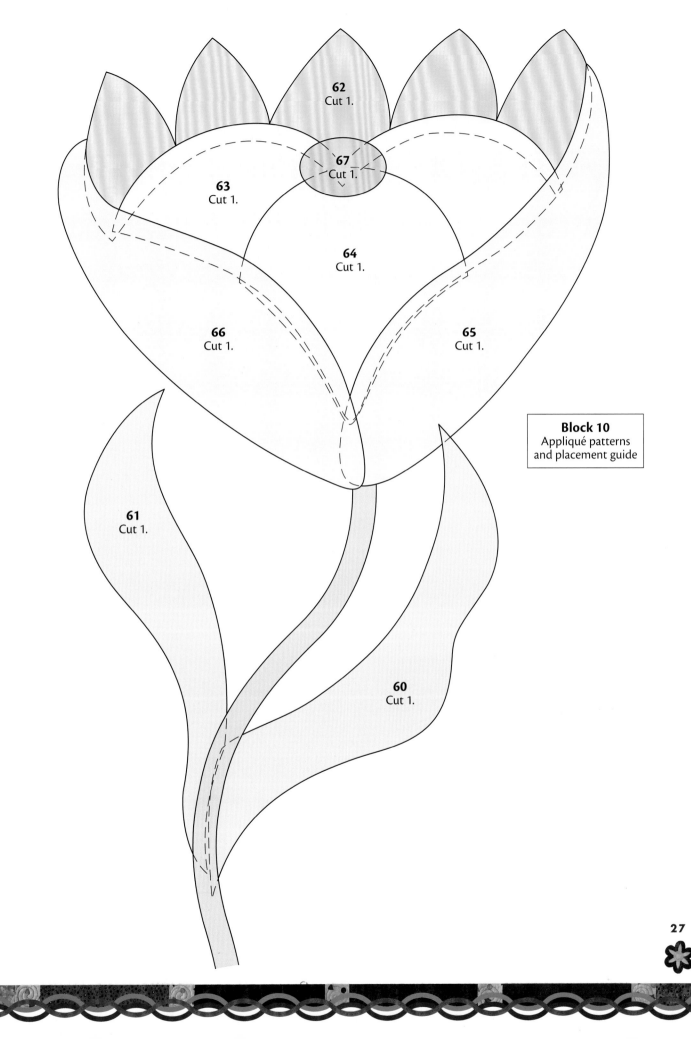

62
Cut 1.

67
Cut 1.

63
Cut 1.

64
Cut 1.

66
Cut 1.

65
Cut 1.

Block 10
Appliqué patterns
and placement guide

61
Cut 1.

60
Cut 1.

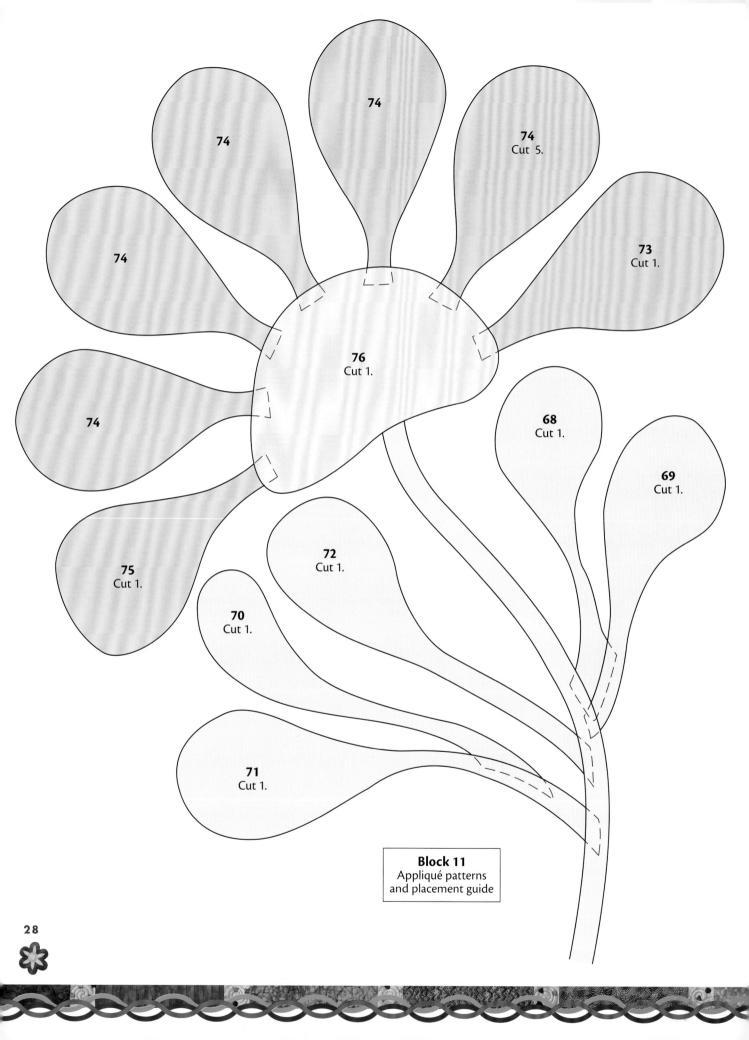

74

74

74
Cut 5.

74

73
Cut 1.

76
Cut 1.

68
Cut 1.

69
Cut 1.

74

72
Cut 1.

75
Cut 1.

70
Cut 1.

71
Cut 1.

Block 11
Appliqué patterns
and placement guide

Block 12
Appliqué patterns
and placement guide

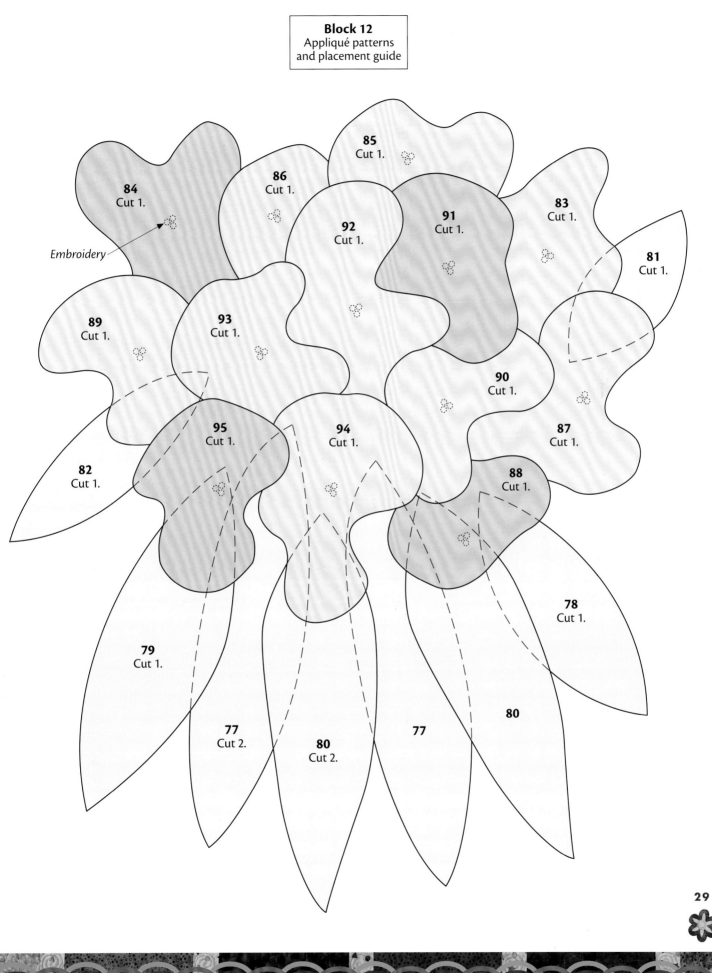

84
Cut 1.

Embroidery

85
Cut 1.

86
Cut 1.

92
Cut 1.

91
Cut 1.

83
Cut 1.

81
Cut 1.

89
Cut 1.

93
Cut 1.

90
Cut 1.

82
Cut 1.

95
Cut 1.

94
Cut 1.

88
Cut 1.

87
Cut 1.

78
Cut 1.

79
Cut 1.

77
Cut 2.

80
Cut 2.

77

80

29

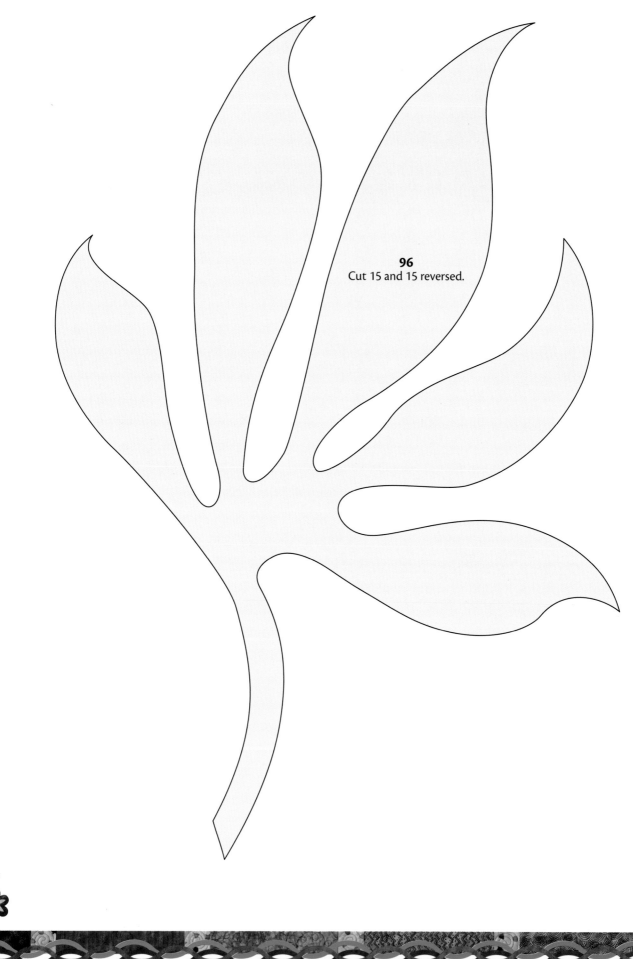

96
Cut 15 and 15 reversed.

DIVINE VINES

How they grow, these lovely vines, without beginning and without end.

MATERIALS

Yardage is based on 42"-wide fabric.

1 yard *each* of light and dark green batiks for leaves

1⅝ yards of orange batik for strips

1⅝ yards of sunflower batik for strips

¼ yard *each* of 5 bright batiks for flowers

½ yard of green batik for binding

3⅓ yards of backing fabric

57" x 60" piece of batting

15 yellow buttons, ¾" diameter, for flower centers

Size 8 pearl cotton for flower centers (optional)

CUTTING

All measurements include ¼"-wide seam allowances. Refer to "Assembling the Quilt" (step 1) before cutting the appliqué pieces.

From the orange batik, cut on the *lengthwise* grain:
3 strips, 9½" x 50½"

From the sunflower batik, cut on the *lengthwise* grain:
4 strips, 5½" x 50½"

From *each* of the light and dark green batik fabrics, cut:
9 of template 1 (18 total)

From *each* of the 5 bright batiks, cut:
3 of template 2 (15 total)

From the green batik for binding, cut:
6 strips, 2" x 42"

ASSEMBLING THE QUILT

1. Choose your favorite method of appliqué and make appliqué templates for the leaves and flowers by tracing the patterns on pages 34 and 35. Refer to "Introduction to Appliqué" on page 119 for details as needed. I used fusible appliqué for this quilt. Cut out the number of each shape indicated in the cutting list.

2. Appliqué all the leaves and then the flowers in position onto the orange batik strips. Refer to the quilt photo on page 33 for placement of leaves and flowers. Position each leaf at a different angle so that they look like they wander up the strip, as leaves do in nature. Appliqué partial leaves at the top and bottom of each strip. After stitching the edges of the leaves with a blanket stitch, I stitched the center vein with a satin stitch before adding the flowers.

Quilt size: 47" x 50"

3. Assemble the quilt top by sewing the four sunflower batik strips and the three appliquéd strips in a vertical arrangement, alternating strips. Press the seam allowances toward the sunflower batik strips.

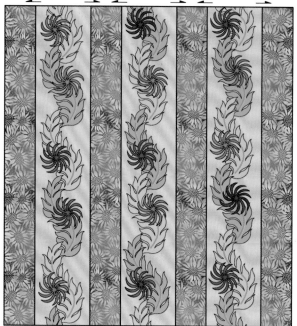

FINISHING THE QUILT

Refer to "Quiltmaking Basics" on page 111 for more details if needed.

1. Mark the quilting design on the quilt top if desired. See the quilting suggestion above right.

2. Layer the quilt top with batting and backing; baste or pin.

3. Quilt by hand or by machine.

4. Use the green batik 2" x 42" strips to bind the edges of the quilt.

5. Sew the fifteen ¾" yellow buttons to the flower centers. I used hand-dyed size 8 pearl cotton to sew the buttons on. I added extra thread tails and left them about ½" long for a wild look.

6. Add a label to the back of your quilt.

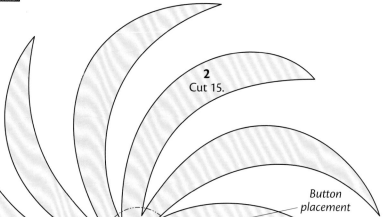

2
Cut 15.

Button placement

Enlarge pattern
on this page 125%.

1
Cut 18.

Satin stitch

MORNING'S GLORY

Tiny butterflies flit among the lush foliage as the sun slowly rises.

MATERIALS

Yardage is based on 42"-wide fabric.

2⅛ yards of dark multicolored print for blocks, sashings, and border 3

1⅞ yards of light multicolored print for blocks, border 1, and binding

1⅞ yards of black print for blocks and border 2

⅓ yard *each* of 5 shades of green hand-dyed fabrics for plants

⅜ yard *each* of 4 shades of gold hand-dyed fabrics for appliqué background

⅜ yard of light orange hand-dyed fabric for blocks

¼ yard of dark orange hand-dyed fabric for blocks

¼ yard of red orange hand-dyed fabric for blocks

3½ yards of fabric for backing

61" x 79" piece of batting

47 butterfly charms, 1" x 1¼"

CUTTING

All measurements include ¼" seam allowances. Cut all lengthwise strips first. Refer to "Appliqué" (step 2) on page 38 before cutting the appliqué pieces.

From the light multicolored print, cut:

2 strips, 2½" x 42" *lengthwise*

2 strips, 2½" x 64" *lengthwise*

4 binding strips, 2" x 67" *lengthwise*

32 squares, 2⅞" x 2⅞ "; cut once diagonally to make 64 half-square triangles

From the red orange hand-dyed fabric, cut:

16 squares, 3⅜" x 3⅜"

From the dark orange hand-dyed fabric, cut:

32 squares, 2½" x 2½"

From the black print, cut:

2 strips, 1" x 46" *lengthwise*

2 strips, 1" x 65" *lengthwise*

40 squares, 2½" x 2½"

Quilt size: 51" x 69" ❀ Block size: 10" x 10"

From the light orange hand-dyed fabric, cut:

8 squares, 5¼" x 5¼"; cut twice diagonally to make 32 quarter-square triangles

From the dark multicolored print, cut:

2 strips, 3½" x 47" *lengthwise*

2 strips, 3½" x 71" *lengthwise*

8 squares, 5¼" x 5¼"; cut twice diagonally to make 32 quarter-square triangles

4 strips, 2½" x 40½"

From the 4 shades of gold hand-dyed fabric, cut a *total* of:

15 rectangles, 4½" x 10½"

30 rectangles, 2½" x 10½"

From *each* of the 5 shades of green hand-dyed fabric, cut:

3 of template 1 (15 total)

ASSEMBLING THE BLOCKS

1. To make unit 1, sew a light multicolored half-square triangle to each side of a red orange 3⅜" square. Sew a dark orange 2½" square to a black print 2½" square, and sew that to the larger square. Make 16 of unit 1.

Unit 1.
Make 16.

2. To make unit 2, sew two light orange quarter-square triangles and two dark multicolored print quarter-square triangles together as shown. Sew a dark orange 2½" square to a black print 2½" square and sew that to the larger square. Make 16 of unit 2.

Unit 2.
Make 16.

3. Construct the block using two each of units 1 and 2. Begin by partially sewing one unit 2 to a black 2½" center square. Add the other three units in a clockwise fashion, and then complete sewing the seam of the first unit 2. Press the seam allowances outward. Make eight blocks.

Unit 1   Unit 2

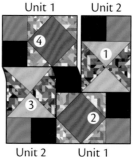 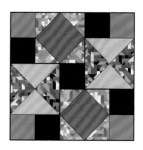

Unit 2   Unit 1

Make 8.

APPLIQUÉ

1. To construct appliqué background strips, sew five gold 4½" x 10½" rectangles and 10 gold 2½" x 10½" rectangles together, alternating the shades of gold as shown. Make three background strips.

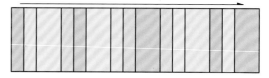

Make 3.

2. Choose your favorite appliqué method and make appliqué templates for the plants by enlarging and tracing the pattern on page 41. Refer to "Introduction to Appliqué" on page 119 for details as needed. Cut out the number of each shape indicated in the cutting list.

3. Appliqué 5 plants to each gold strip, overlapping them as desired. Refer to the quilt photo on page 37 for placement guidance.

ASSEMBLING THE QUILT

1. Assemble the blocks into two horizontal rows of four blocks each; sew the blocks together and press.

2. Assemble the quilt center by alternating the appliqué rows and the block rows with the four dark multicolored print 2½" x 40½" sashing strips.

3. To add the top and bottom strips of border 1, measure across the center of the quilt. Trim the two light multicolored 2½" x 42" strips to this measurement and sew them to the top and bottom of the quilt. Press the seam allowances toward the border strips.

4. To add the side borders, measure lengthwise through the center of the quilt, including the top and bottom strips. Trim the light multicolored 2½" x 64" side border strips to this measurement and sew them to the sides of the quilt; press.

5. Repeat steps 3 and 4 to add borders 2 and 3.

FINISHING THE QUILT

Refer to "Quiltmaking Basics" on page 111 for more details if needed.

1. Mark the quilting design on the quilt top if desired. See the quilting suggestion on page 40.

2. Layer the quilt top with batting and backing; baste or pin.

3. Quilt by hand or by machine.

4. Use the light multicolored 2" x 67" strips to bind the edges of the quilt.

5. Whimsically scatter the butterfly charms among the plants. Sew in position.

6. Add a label to the back of your quilt.

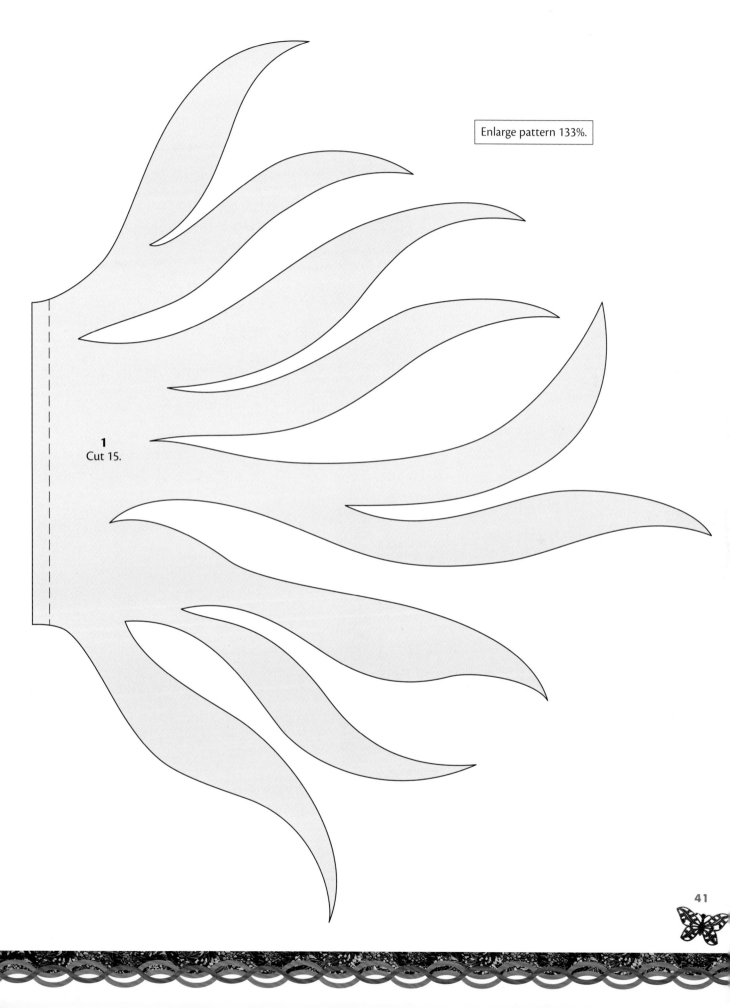

Enlarge pattern 133%.

1
Cut 15.

FALLING WATER

Waterfalls abound, cool and refreshing.

MATERIALS

Yardage is based on 42"-wide fabric.

1⅞ yards of large-scale blue green jungle print 1 for blocks and borders

½ yard of large-scale blue print for blocks

½ yard of green jungle print for blocks

½ yard of large-scale blue green jungle print 2 for blocks

⅛ yard *each* of 2 light blue prints for blocks

⅛ yard *each* of 2 lime green prints for blocks

½ yard of black fabric for binding

3½ yards of fabric for backing

59" x 71" piece of batting

24 yards of blue green, sheer, 1½"-wide polyester ribbon

Miscellaneous buttons, shells, shiny plastic round disks, iron-on crystals, etc., to decorate ribbons

4 skeins of 6-strand embroidery floss in a complementary color

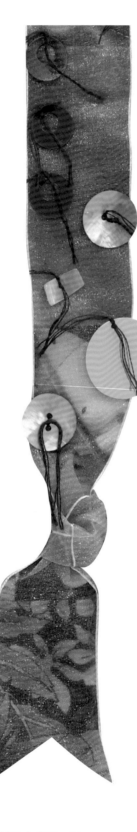

CUTTING

All measurements include ¼" seam allowances. Cut all lengthwise strips first.

From the large-scale blue green jungle print 1, cut:

2 strips, 7" x 38" *lengthwise*

2 strips, 7" x 63" *lengthwise*

12 rectangles, 4½" x 8½"

24 rectangles, 2½" x 4½"

From the large-scale blue print, cut:

6 strips, 2½" x 42"; cut into 48 rectangles, 2½" x 4½"

From the green jungle print, cut:

5 strips, 2½" x 42"; cut into:

24 rectangles, 2½" x 4½"

24 squares, 2½" x 2½"

From the large-scale blue green jungle print 2, cut:

5 strips, 2½" x 42"; cut into:

24 rectangles, 2½" x 4½"

24 squares, 2½" x 2½"

From *each* of the 2 light blue prints for blocks, cut:

12 squares, 2½" x 2½" (24 total)

From *each* of the 2 lime green prints, cut:

12 squares, 2½" x 2½" (24 total)

From the black fabric, cut:

6 strips, 2" x 42"

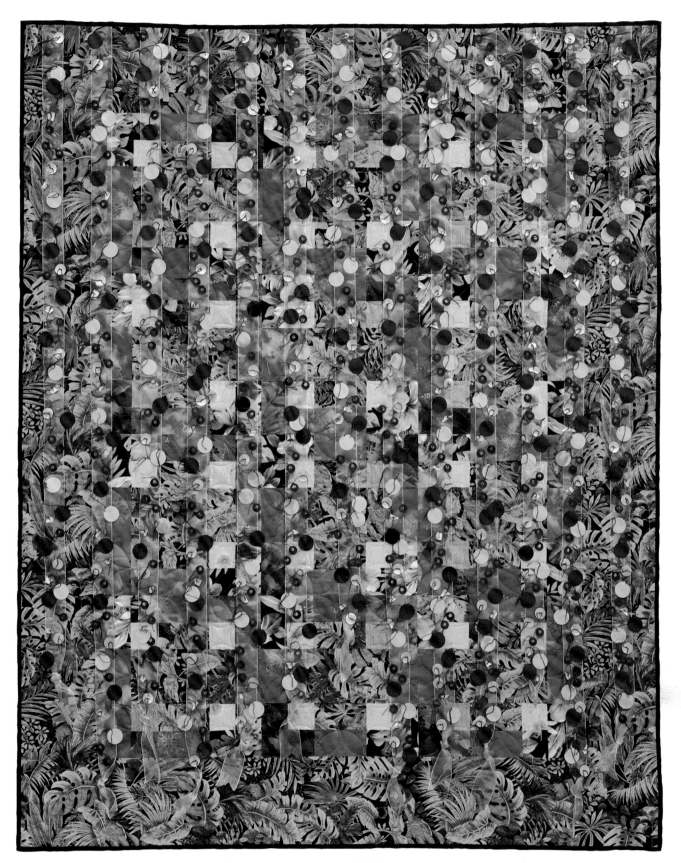

Quilt size: 49" x 61"   ❀   Block size: 12" x 12"

ASSEMBLING THE QUILT

1. Construct 12 blocks for the center of the quilt, assembling them as shown in the block layout. Press the seam allowances, following the arrows in the diagram.

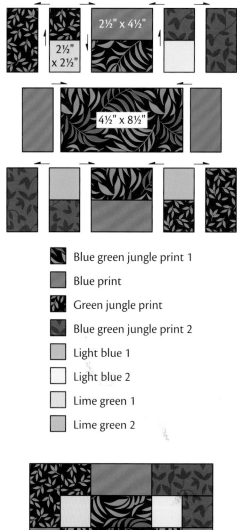

Blue green jungle print 1

Blue print

Green jungle print

Blue green jungle print 2

Light blue 1

Light blue 2

Lime green 1

Lime green 2

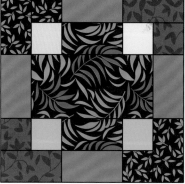

Make 12.

2. Assemble the quilt center by sewing together four horizontal rows of three blocks each. Press the seam allowances in opposite directions from row to row. Sew the rows together.

3. To add the top and bottom borders, measure across the center of the quilt. Trim both large-scale blue green jungle print 7" x 38" strips to that measurement and sew them to the top and bottom of the quilt. Press the seam allowances toward the border strips.

4. To add the side borders, measure lengthwise through the center of the quilt, including the top and bottom border strips. Trim the large-scale blue green jungle print 7" x 63" strips to that measurement and sew them to the sides of the quilt; press.

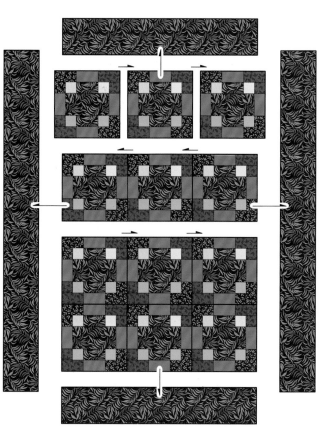

FINISHING THE QUILT

Refer to "Quiltmaking Basics" on page 111 for more details if needed.

1. Mark the quilting design on the quilt top if desired. See the quilting suggestion below.

2. Layer the quilt top with batting and backing; baste or pin.

3. Quilt by hand or by machine.

4. Cut the ribbon into 13 pieces, each 65" long. Just before binding the edges of the quilt, baste the ends of the ribbon across the top of the quilt, leaving about 2" between each piece.

5. Use the black 2" x 42" strips to bind the edges of the quilt.

6. Add a label to the back of your quilt.

7. Decorate the ribbon lengths with shiny items of your choice. Use two strands of a 6-strand embroidery thread to attach the items. Leave long tails when trimming the thread. Knot the end of each ribbon strip at varying lengths and trim. Refer to "Embellishments" on page 124 for additional information.

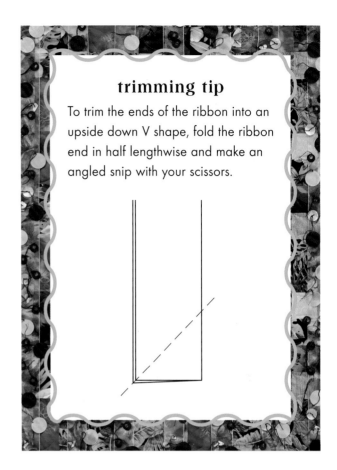

trimming tip

To trim the ends of the ribbon into an upside down V shape, fold the ribbon end in half lengthwise and make an angled snip with your scissors.

STARRY NIGHT

The jungle is a busy, happy place at night. Listen closely, and you'll hear the joy.

MATERIALS

Yardage is based on 42"-wide fabric.

2⅛ yards of blue print for inner border*

1¼ yards of multicolored batik for blocks and outer border

1¼ yards of black print for appliqué background and binding

1 yard of multicolored print for sashing**

½ yard each of 2 green prints for leaves

⅜ yard each of 3 orange, 2 pink, 1 purple, 1 light purple, 1 green, 1 multicolored, and 1 yellow print for flowers, blocks, and outer border

¼ yard of green print for bias stems

5½ yards of fabric for backing

66" x 94" piece of batting

13 yards of ⅜"-wide multicolored trim

30 yellow beads, ½" long, for flowers

81 small bells (⅜") and 6 large bells (2" long)

Yellow embroidery floss

If you prefer to cut the inner border strips crosswise and piece them, ⅝ yard is enough.

**If your fabric is not at least 40½" wide after prewashing and removing selvages, you will need 1⅓ yards.*

CUTTING

All measurements include ¼" seam allowances. Refer to "Assembling the Quilt" (steps 1 and 2) on page 48 before cutting the appliqué pieces.

From the green print for bias stems, cut:
½"-wide bias strips to total 78"

From the black print, cut:
2 strips, 10½" x 40½"
8 binding strips, 2" x 42"

From *each* of the 3 orange prints, cut:
15 of template 2 (45 total)

From *each* of the 2 pink prints, cut:
15 of template 1 (30 total)

From the purple print, cut:
15 of template 2

From the green print for blocks and border, cut:
15 of template 1
6 of template 4
4 of template 5

From the yellow print, cut:
15 of template 1

Quilt size: 56" x 84" ❁ Block size: 8" x 8"

From the remainder of the orange, pink, purple, light purple, green, multicolored, and yellow prints for pieced border and flowers, cut a total of:

116 rectangles, 2½" x 6½"

30 of template 6 (matching groups of 5)

20 of template 7 (matching groups of 5)

From the 2 green prints for leaves, cut:

6 of template 3

6 of template 3 reversed

From the multicolored batik for blocks and outer border, cut:

15 squares, 4⅛" x 4⅛"

60 of template 1 reversed

4 squares, 6½" x 6½"

From the multicolored print, cut:

6 strips, 4½" x 40½"

From the blue print, cut on the *lengthwise* grain:

2 strips, 2½" x 40½"

2 strips, 2½" x 72½"

ASSEMBLING THE QUILT

1. Refer to "Making Bias Stems and Vines" on page 123 to make ¼"-wide bias strips from the green print ½"-wide bias strips.

2. Choose your favorite appliqué method and make appliqué templates for the leaves and flowers by tracing the patterns on pages 52 and 53. Refer to "Introduction to Appliqué" on page 119 for details as needed. Cut out the number of each shape indicated in the cutting list.

3. Appliqué all leaves, bias stems, and flowers to the black print 10½" x 40½" strips, referring to the placement diagram below. Stem stitch the flower stamens using 2 strands of 6-strand embroidery floss. Refer to "Embroidery Stitches" on page 120.

4. Construct 15 identical pieced blocks using the 4⅛" squares and the patches cut using templates 1 and 2. Refer to the diagram for the piecing order. Before sewing, arrange the cut pieces on top of the pattern so you won't get confused about which pieces go where. Piece the three sections, and then sew the sections together. Mark the seam intersections and use a pin to match them to align the angled pieces correctly. Press the seam allowances as shown in the diagram.

Make 15.

5. Sew the 15 blocks into three horizontal rows of five blocks each.

6. Alternate multicolored print 4½" x 40½" sashing strips with the block and appliqué strips as shown

Appliqué placement

in the quilt layout. Sew the strips together. Press the seam allowances toward the sashing strips.

7. Sew the blue print 2½" x 40½" strips to the top and bottom of the quilt. Press seam allowances toward the border strips.

8. Sew the blue print 2½" x 72½" strips to the sides of the quilt; press.

9. Construct two strips consisting of 22 bright-colored 2½" x 6½" rectangles, alternating colors. Press the seam allowances in one direction. Sew the strips to the top and bottom of the quilt. Press the seam allowances toward the blue print strips.

Make 2.

10. Construct two strips consisting of 36 bright-colored 2½" x 6½" rectangles; press. Sew a multicolored

batik 6½" square to the end of each strip; press. Sew the strips to the sides of the quilt; press.

Make 2.

FINISHING THE QUILT

Refer to "Quiltmaking Basics" on page 111 for more details if needed.

1. Mark the quilting design on the quilt top if desired. See the quilting suggestion on page 51.

2. Layer the quilt top with batting and backing; baste or pin.

3. Quilt by hand or by machine.

4. Use the black print 2" x 42" strips to bind the edges of the quilt.

5. Sew the ½" yellow beads to the stamens of the flowers.

6. For each star block, cut 3 pieces of trim 6" long. Knot the top and sew or knot one ⅜" bell to the bottom of each strip. Make 15 units. Sew the units to the top point of each star block.

7. Cut three pieces of trim 9" long and knot a 2" bell in the center of the strips. Sew or knot six ⅜" bells to the ends of the strips. Make six units. Evenly space the bell units along the bottom edge of the quilt. Sew in position.

8. Add a label to the back of your quilt.

Small bells at the top of the block

Bell unit at the bottom edge of the quilt

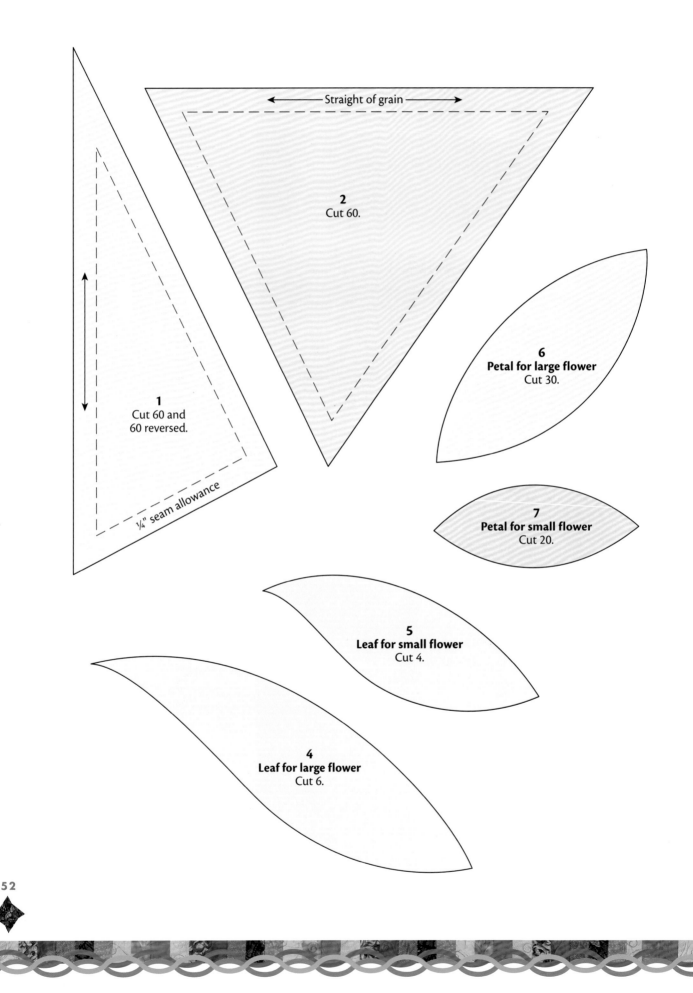

Straight of grain

2
Cut 60.

1
Cut 60 and
60 reversed.

¼" seam allowance

6
Petal for large flower
Cut 30.

7
Petal for small flower
Cut 20.

5
Leaf for small flower
Cut 4.

4
Leaf for large flower
Cut 6.

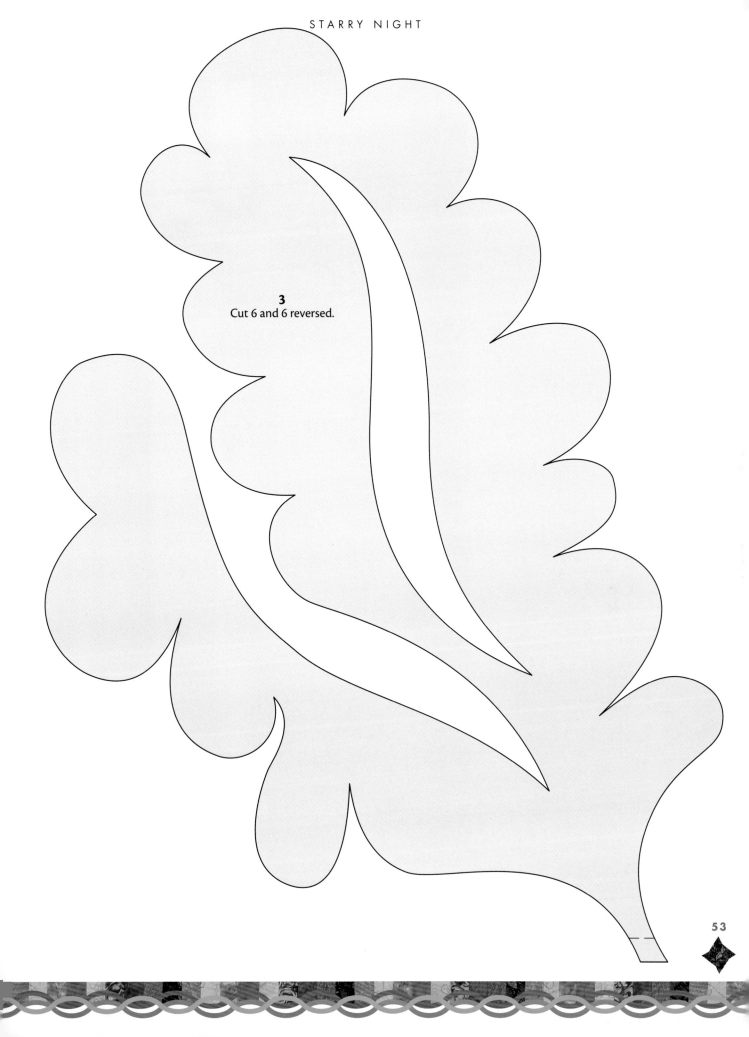

3
Cut 6 and 6 reversed.

ISLAND TREASURES

The treasure of the islands, no money can buy.

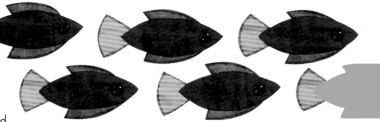

MATERIALS

Yardage is based on 42"-wide fabric.

2⅛ yards of multicolored tropical print for blocks, appliquéd border, and outer border

1⅞ yards of yellow print 1 for blocks and appliquéd border

1⅓ yards of red print 1 for blocks, inner border, and appliquéd border

¾ yard of black print for blocks, appliquéd border, and binding

½ yard of green print 1 for block 10 and appliquéd border

⅜ yard of green print 2 for block 7 and appliquéd border

⅜ yard of blue print for blocks 1 and 6 and appliquéd border

⅓ yard of gold print for blocks, border strip, and appliquéd border

⅓ yard *each* of 7 teal prints for blocks, border strip, and appliquéd border

⅓ yard *each* of 2 yellow prints for blocks and appliquéd border

¼ yard *each* of 6 green prints for blocks and appliquéd border

¼ yard *each* of 3 red prints for blocks and appliquéd border

Scrap of light orange fabric for rooster

3½ yards of fabric for backing

59" x 77" piece of batting

5 black buttons, ⅜" diameter, for eyes

2 small black beads for eyes

1 skein of orange 6-strand embroidery floss

CUTTING

All measurements include ¼-wide" seam allowances. Cut all lengthwise strips first.

From the multicolored tropical print, cut:
2 strips, 4" x 42½" *lengthwise*
2 strips, 4" x 67½" *lengthwise*
2 rectangles, 1½" x 6½" (block 1)
2 strips, 1½" x 18½" (block 1)
2 rectangles, 1½" x 4½" (block 3)
2 strips, 1½" x 16½" (block 3)
2 strips, 1½" x 12½" (block 6)
2 strips, 1½" x 16½" (block 6)
2 rectangles, 1½" x 2½" (block 8)
2 rectangles, 1½" x 4½" (block 8)

From the yellow print 1, cut:
2 strips, 6½" x 30½" *lengthwise*
2 strips, 6½" x 60½" *lengthwise*
1 rectangle, 4½" x 14½" (block 3)

From the red print 1, cut on the *lengthwise* grain:
2 strips, 1½" x 30½"
2 strips, 1½" x 42½"

From the black print, cut:
6 strips, 2" x 42"

From the 2 yellow prints, cut a *total* of:
1 rectangle, 8½" x 14½" (block 5)
2 rectangles, 4" x 5" (block 4)
1 rectangle, 10½" x 12½" (block 9)

Quilt size: 49" x 67"

From the 3 red prints, cut a *total* of:

6 rectangles, 1¼" x 4" (block 4)

From the green print 2, cut:

1 rectangle, 6½" x 12½" (block 7)

From the green print 1, cut:

1 rectangle, 12½" x 14½" (block 10)

From *1 of the 6* green prints, cut:

1 rectangle, 4½" x 30½" (block 4)

From *1 of the 7* teal prints, cut:

2 strips, 1½" x 30½"

5 rectangles, 3" x 4" (block 4)

1 square, 2½" x 2½" (block 8)

From the 7 teal prints, cut a *total* of:

7 squares, 4½" x 4½" (block 2)

From the gold print, cut:

2 strips, 1½" x 30½"

From the blue print, cut:

1 rectangle, 6½" x 16½" (block 1)

1 rectangle, 10½" x 16½" (block 6)

APPLIQUÉ CUTTING KEY

Refer to "Appliquéing the Blocks" (steps 2 and 3) on page 57 before cutting the appliqué pieces.

From the remainder of the 8 green prints, cut a *total* of:

½"-wide bias strips to total 30"

4 of template 1 (matching set)

4 of template 2 (matching set)

4 of template 3 (matching set)

13 of template 6

4 of template 17

1 of template 18

2 of template 19

5 of template 51

14 of template 53

From the remainder of the 3 red prints, cut a *total* of:

4 of template 4 (matching set)

2 of template 5

2 of template 12

2 of template 14

2 of template 16

1 of template 34

1 of template 42

5 of template 51

From the remainder of yellow print 1, cut:

2 of template 5

1 *each* of templates 20–29

From the remainder of red print 1, cut:

1 *each* of templates 5, 35, and 38

8 of template 10

2 *each* of templates 11, 13, 15, and 51

From the remainder of the 2 yellow prints, cut a *total* of:

2 of template 5

7 of template 53

From the remainder of black print, cut:

1 *each* of templates 7, 30, 31, 32, and 51

From the remainder of multicolored tropical print, cut:

5 of template 9

26 of template 52

From the remainder of gold print, cut:

1 of template 33

1 of template 40

2 of template 51

From the scrap of light orange, cut:

1 *each* of templates 36, 37, and 39

From the remainder of the 7 teal prints, cut a *total* of:

1 of template 41

1 of template 43

1 of template 44

1 of template 45 and 1 reversed

1 of template 46 and 1 reversed

1 of template 47 and 1 reversed

1 of template 48

1 of template 49

1 of template 50

10 of template 51

5 of template 53

From the remainder of blue print, cut:

1 of template 51

APPLIQUÉING THE BLOCKS

1. Sew the two yellow 4" x 5" rectangles, the six red 1¼" x 4" rectangles, and the five teal 3" x 4" rectangles for block 4 in a strip as shown. Press the seam allowances toward the red strips. Cut one of template 8 on page 61 from this strip.

2. Refer to "Making Bias Stems and Vines" on page 123 to make ¼"-wide bias strips from the green print ½"-wide bias strips.

3. Choose your favorite appliqué method and make appliqué templates for the items in blocks 1–10 and the appliquéd border by tracing the patterns on pages 60–67. Refer to "Introduction to Appliqué" on page 119 for details as needed. Cut out the number of each shape indicated in the "Appliqué Cutting Key."

4. **Block 1.** Appliqué the fish (templates 1–4) to the blue 6½" x 16½" background rectangle. Refer to the photograph on page 55 for placement guidance. Sew the multicolored 1½" x 6½" rectangles to the sides. Press the seam allowances toward the rectangles. Add the multicolored 1½" x 18½" strips to the top and bottom; press.

5. **Block 2.** Appliqué a star (template 5) to each of the seven teal 4½" squares.

6. **Block 3.** Appliqué the bias stem and then the leaves (template 6) to the yellow print 4½" x 14½" rectangle. Sew the multicolored 1½" x 4½" rectangles to the top and bottom. Press the seam allowances toward the rectangles. Add the multicolored 1½" x 16½" strips to the sides; press.

7. **Block 4.** Appliqué the snake (cut in step 1), tongue, circles, and diamonds (templates 7–10) to the green print 4½" x 30½" background rectangle.

8. **Block 5.** Appliqué the bias stem and then the leaves and flowers (templates 11–19) to the yellow 8½" x 14½" background rectangle.

Block 5 appliqué placement

9. **Block 6.** Appliqué the sun and palm trees (templates 20–32) to the blue 10½" x 16½" background rectangle. Sew the multicolored 1½" x 16½" strips to the top and bottom. Press the seam allowances toward the strips. Add the multicolored 1½" x 12½" strips to the sides; press.

Block 6 appliqué placement

10. **Block 7.** Appliqué the gecko (template 33) to the green 6½" x 12½" background rectangle.

11. **Block 8.** Sew a multicolored tropical print 1½" x 2½" rectangle to the top and bottom of the teal 2½" square. Press the seam allowances toward the rectangles. Sew the multicolored 1½" x 4½" rectangles to the sides; press. Appliqué the small heart (template 34) to the center of the block.

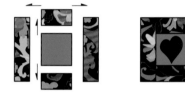

12. **Block 9.** Appliqué the rooster (templates 35–43) to the yellow 10½" x 12½" background rectangle. Embroider the feet and beak onto the rooster.

13. **Block 10.** Appliqué the tropical plant (templates 44–50) to the green 12½" x 14½" background rectangle. Refer to the photograph on page 55 for placement guidance.

ASSEMBLING THE QUILT

1. Construct the quilt center in sections. You will need to sew the sections together and then join them using a partial seam as shown in the quilt layout diagram. Follow the sequence below.
   - Sew two of block 2 together and sew to block 1.
   - Sew two of block 2 together and sew to block 5.
   - Sew block 6 to block 7.
   - Sew three of block 2 together and sew to block 9. Sew this section to block 10.
   - Sew the block 2/9/10 section to the block 6/7 section.
   - Sew block 8 to block 4.
   - Sew block section 4/8 to block section 5/2/2 with a partial seam.
   - Sew block section 1/2/2 to the top of the previous unit.

- Sew block 3 to the right side.
- Sew the block section 6/7/2/9/10 to the bottom of the previous unit.
- Complete the seam of the block 4/8 section.

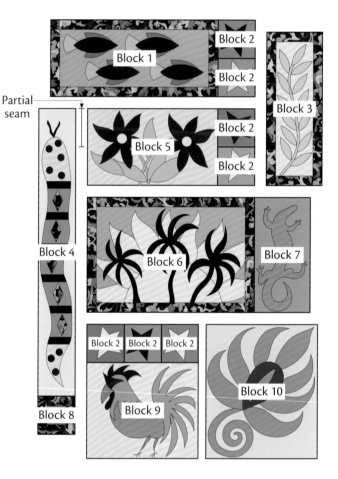

2. Sew the red print 1½" x 42½" strips to the sides of the quilt; press the seam allowances toward the border strips.

3. Sew the red print 1½" x 30½" strips to the top and bottom of the quilt; press.

4. Sew the gold print 1½" x 30½" strips to the top and bottom of the quilt; press.

5. Sew the teal print 1½" x 30½" strips to the top and bottom of the quilt; press.

6. With a pencil, lightly mark five sections 6" wide on the two yellow print 6½" x 30½" strips. Remember to leave ¼" seam allowances on each end. Appliqué five border units (templates 51–53 on page 67) to each strip.

7. Sew the top and bottom borders to the quilt. Press the seam allowances toward border 1 to eliminate bulk.

8. Mark eight 6"-wide sections on the two yellow print 6½" x 60½" strips, leaving a 6¼" space on each end. Appliqué eight border units to each strip. Sew the borders to the sides of the quilt and press.

9. Sew the multicolored tropical print 4" x 42½" strips to the top and bottom of the quilt. Press the seam allowances toward the border strips. Sew the multicolored tropical print 4" x 67½" strips to the sides of the quilt; press.

FINISHING THE QUILT

Refer to "Quiltmaking Basics" on page 111 for more details if needed.

1. Mark the quilting design on the quilt top if desired. See the quilting suggestion below.

2. Layer the quilt top with batting and backing; baste or pin.

3. Quilt by hand or by machine.

4. Use the black print 2" x 42" strips to bind the edges of the quilt.

5. Add a label to the back of your quilt.

6. Sew four ⅜" black buttons for fish eyes in block 1 and one for the rooster's eye in block 9. Sew two small black beads for the gecko's eyes in block 7.

59

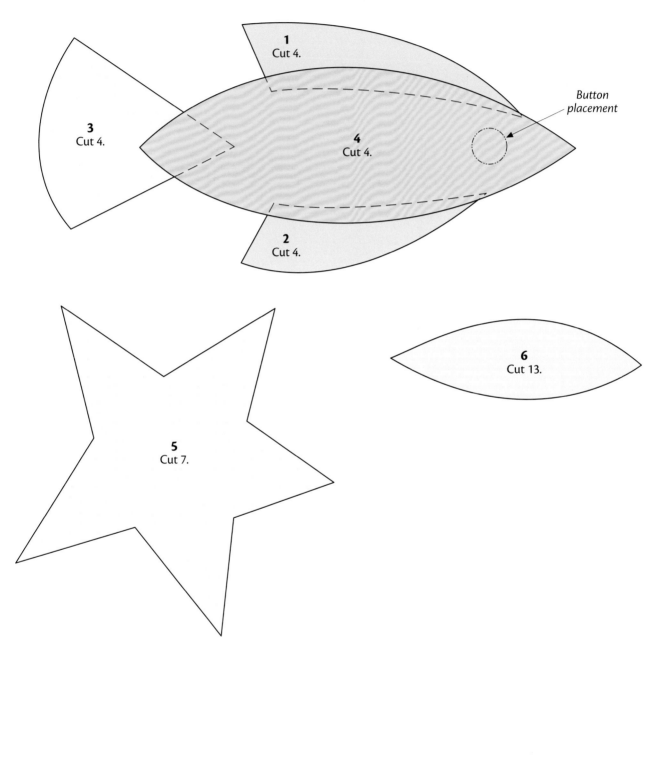

1
Cut 4.

3
Cut 4.

Button
placement

4
Cut 4.

2
Cut 4.

6
Cut 13.

5
Cut 7.

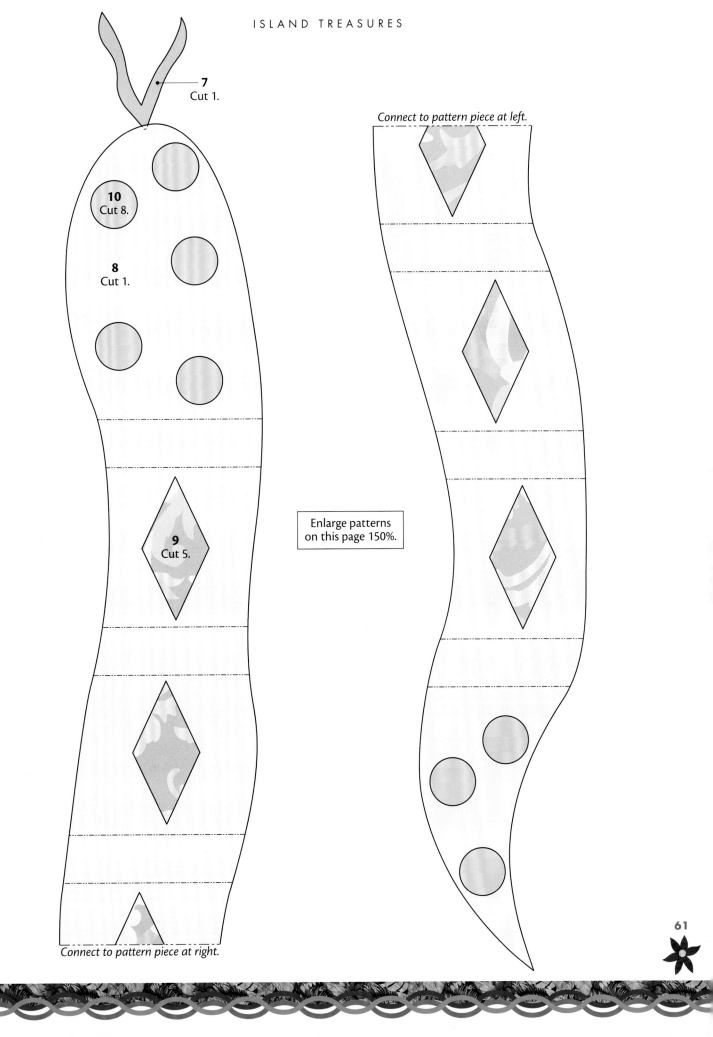

7
Cut 1.

10
Cut 8.

8
Cut 1.

9
Cut 5.

Connect to pattern piece at right.

Connect to pattern piece at left.

Enlarge patterns
on this page 150%.

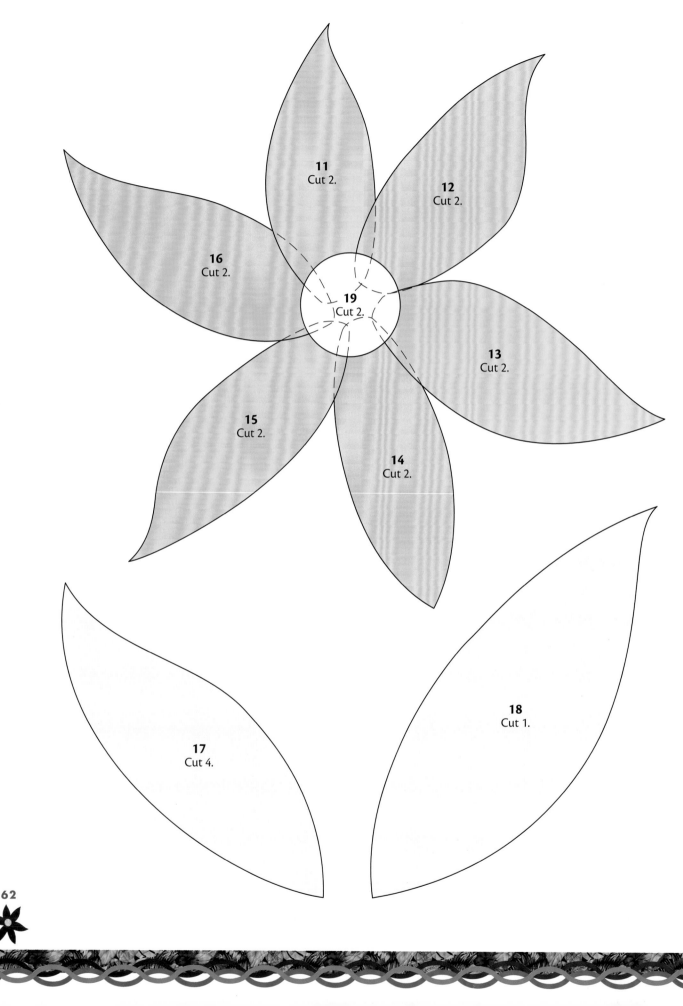

11
Cut 2.

12
Cut 2.

16
Cut 2.

19
Cut 2.

13
Cut 2.

15
Cut 2.

14
Cut 2.

18
Cut 1.

17
Cut 4.

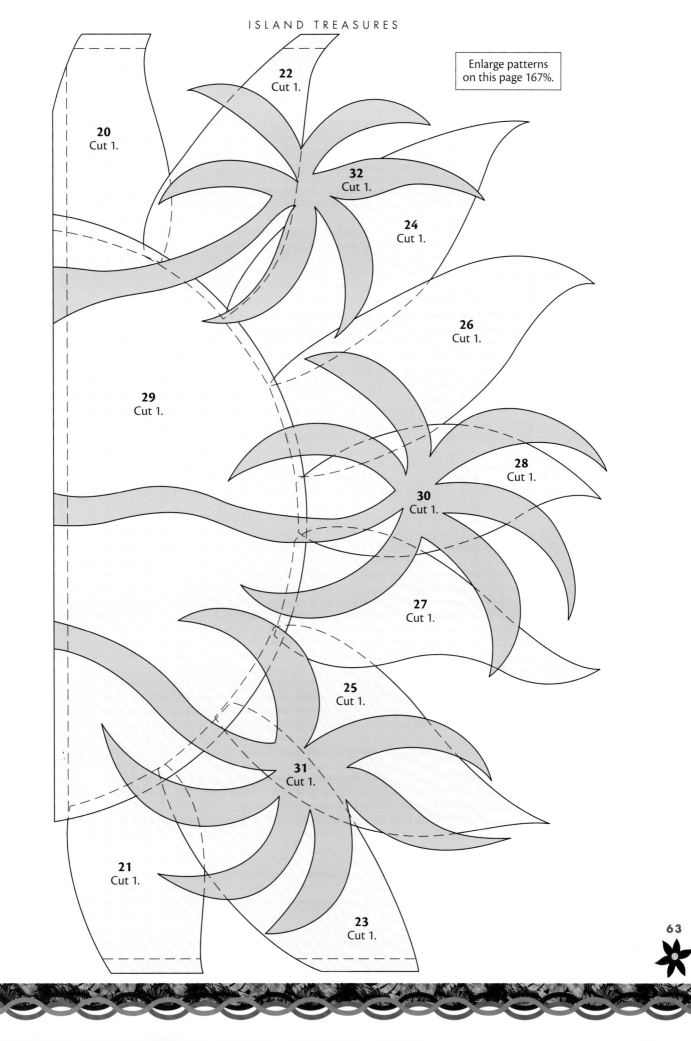

Enlarge patterns
on this page 167%.

22
Cut 1.

20
Cut 1.

32
Cut 1.

24
Cut 1.

26
Cut 1.

29
Cut 1.

28
Cut 1.

30
Cut 1.

27
Cut 1.

25
Cut 1.

31
Cut 1.

21
Cut 1.

23
Cut 1.

Bead placement

34
Cut 1.

33
Cut 1.

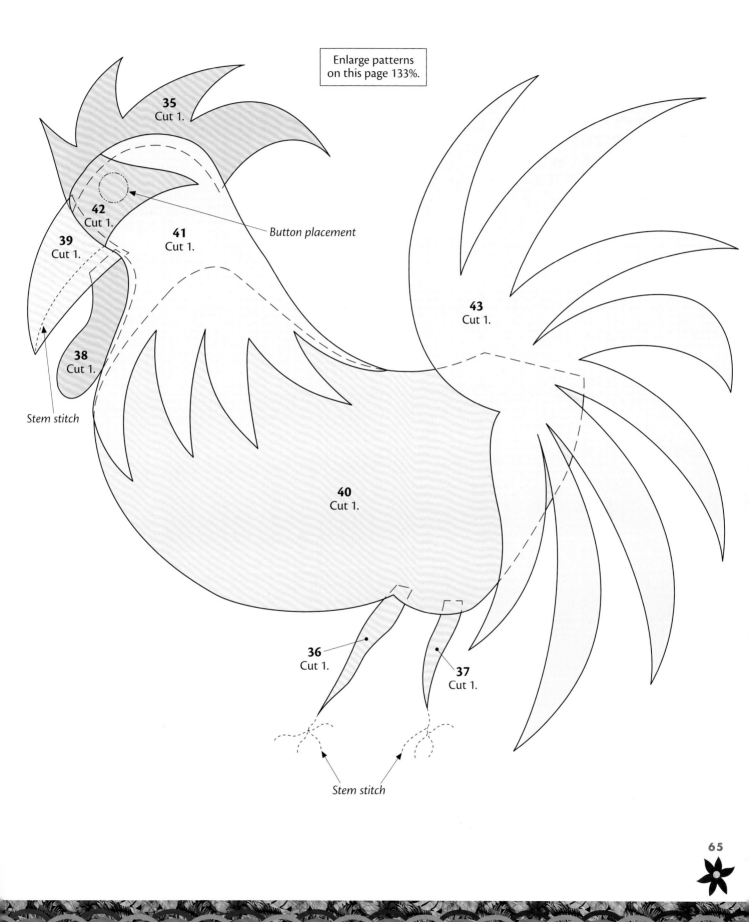

Enlarge patterns
on this page 133%.

35
Cut 1.

42
Cut 1.

Button placement

41
Cut 1.

39
Cut 1.

38
Cut 1.

Stem stitch

43
Cut 1.

40
Cut 1.

36
Cut 1.

37
Cut 1.

Stem stitch

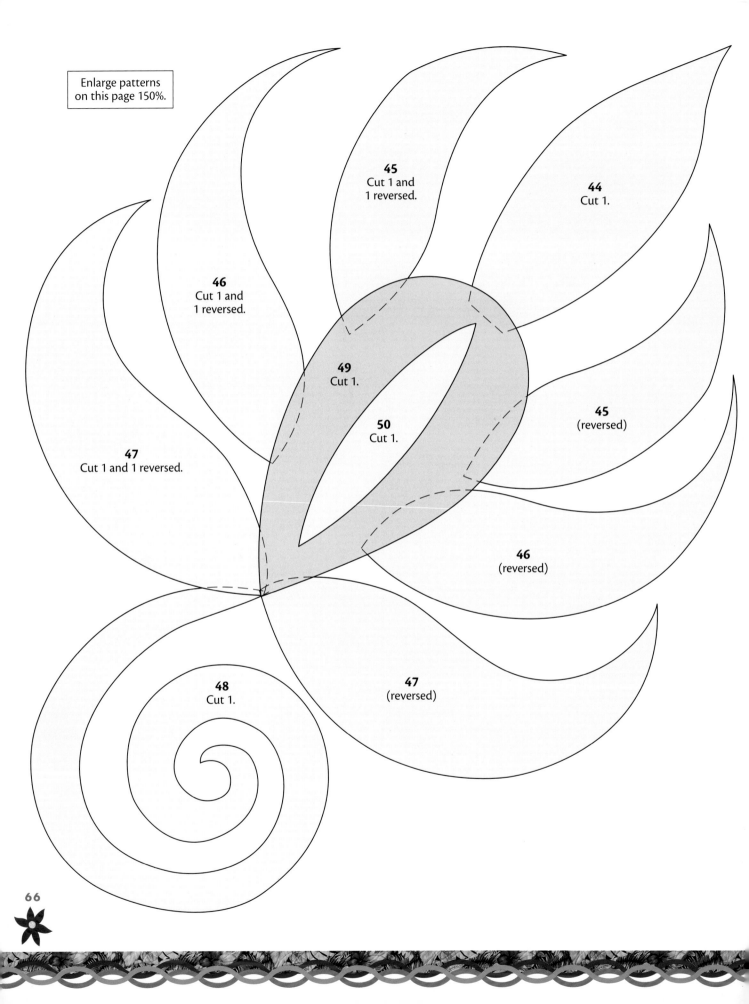

Enlarge patterns
on this page 150%.

45
Cut 1 and
1 reversed.

44
Cut 1.

46
Cut 1 and
1 reversed.

49
Cut 1.

50
Cut 1.

45
(reversed)

47
Cut 1 and 1 reversed.

46
(reversed)

48
Cut 1.

47
(reversed)

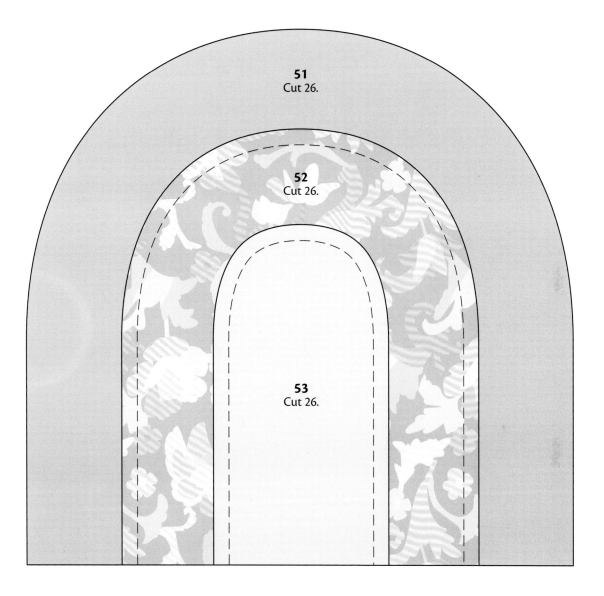

51
Cut 26.

52
Cut 26.

53
Cut 26.

NATURAL BEAUTIES

Tropical prints and big luscious flowers bring the islands to mind.

MATERIALS

Yardage is based on 42"-wide fabric.

⅞ yard of gold print for appliquéd center blocks, corner blocks, and outer border

⅝ yard of multicolored print for inner border

½ yard of gold-and-green print for outer border

⅜ yard of brown print 1 for middle border

¼ yard *each* of teal print 1, brown print 2, medium green print, dark green print 1, dark green print 2, and orange print 1 for center blocks and outer border

⅛ yard *each* of teal print 2 and orange print 2 for center blocks and outer border

⅛ yard of light gold print for outer border

½ yard of brown print 3 for binding

3¼ yards of fabric for backing

58" x 58" piece of batting

4 orange buttons, ½" diameter, for flower centers

Small gold beads for flowers

Size 8 orange pearl cotton

1 skein of orange 6-strand embroidery floss

CUTTING

All measurements include ¼-wide" seam allowances. Refer to "Assembling the Blocks" (steps 2 and 3) on page 70 before cutting the appliqué pieces.

From the gold print, cut:
4 squares, 12½" x 12½"
4 squares, 6½" x 6½"
6 rectangles, 2" x 6½"

From the dark green print 1, cut:
½"-wide bias strips to total 80"
6 rectangles, 2" x 6½"

From the medium green print, cut:
6 rectangles, 2" x 6½"
8 each of templates 3 and 4
4 of template 5

From the dark green print 2, cut:
4 of template 6
8 of template 7
4 of template 8

Quilt size: 48" x 48" ❀ Block size: 12" x 12"

From the orange print 1, cut:
6 rectangles, 2" x 6½"
2 each of templates 9–13

From the orange print 2, cut:
2 each of templates 9–13

From the teal print 1, cut:
6 rectangles, 2" x 6½"
4 of template 1

From the brown print 2, cut:
6 rectangles, 2" x 6½"
4 of template 2

From the teal print 2, cut:
2 squares, 2⅞" x 2⅞"; cut once diagonally to make
    4 half-square triangles
6 rectangles, 2" x 6½"

From the multicolored print, cut:
2 strips, 4½" x 24½"
2 strips, 4½" x 32½"

From the brown print 1, cut:
2 strips, 2½" x 32½"
2 strips, 2½" x 36½"

From the gold-and-green print, cut:
2 strips, 6½" x 36½"

From the light gold print, cut:
6 rectangles, 2" x 6½"

From the brown print 3, cut:
5 strips, 2" x 42"

ASSEMBLING THE BLOCKS

1. Measure down 6¼" on two sides of the four gold print 12½" squares and make a mark. Align a ruler with the marks and cut away the corner triangle on each square.

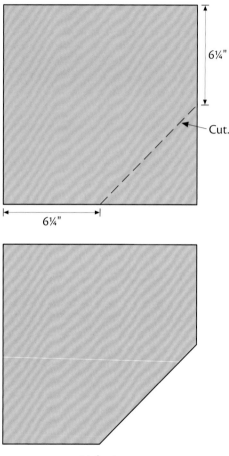

Make 4.

2. Refer to "Making Bias Stems and Vines" on page 123 to make ¼"-wide bias strips from the dark green print ½"-wide bias strips.

3. Choose your favorite appliqué method and make appliqué templates for the leaves and flowers by tracing the patterns on pages 74 and 75. Refer to "Introduction to Appliqué" on page 119 for details as needed. Cut out the number of each shape indicated in the cutting list.

4. Appliqué bias stems, leaves, and flowers in position on the four center blocks using the photograph on page 69 and the diagram below as a guide for placement. Appliqué the four gold print 6½" squares (the corner blocks of the outer border) using the pattern on page 74 as a placement guide. Complete all embroidery as well.

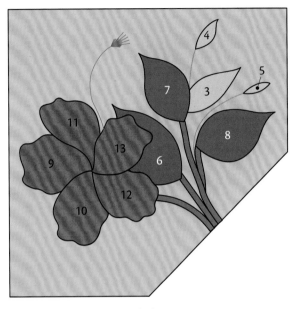

Appliqué placement

5. Sew one template 1, one template 2, and one teal print half-square triangle to each of the four gold print center blocks as shown. Press the seam allowances toward the center in two blocks and away from the center in the other two blocks so that the seams will butt together when joined.

Make 4.

ASSEMBLING THE QUILT

1. Sew the four gold print center blocks together so that the pieced corners form the center square; press.

2. Sew the multicolored print 4½" x 24½" strips to the top and bottom of the center square. Press the seam allowances toward the border strips.

3. Sew the multicolored print 4½" x 32½" strips to the sides of the center square; press.

4. Sew the brown print 1 strips, 2½" x 32½", to the top and bottom of the quilt; press. Sew the brown print 2½" x 36½" strips to the sides of the quilt; press.

5. Use the 2" x 6½" rectangles to make two borders of 24 rectangles each. Press the seam allowances in one direction.

Make 2.

6. Sew the pieced strips to the top and bottom of the quilt. Press the seam allowances toward the middle border to prevent bulk.

7. Sew one appliquéd 6½" square to each end of the two gold-and-green print 6½" x 36½" strips. Press the seam allowances toward the appliquéd squares.

8. Sew the strips to the sides of the quilt; press.

FINISHING THE QUILT

Refer to "Quiltmaking Basics" on page 111 for more details if needed.

1. Mark the quilting design on the quilt top if desired. See the quilting suggestion below.

2. Layer the quilt top with batting and backing; baste or pin.

3. Quilt by hand or by machine.

4. Use the brown print 3 strips, 2" x 42", to bind the edges of the quilt.

5. Add a label to the back of your quilt.

6. Sew the four ½" orange buttons and the small gold beads on the flowers.

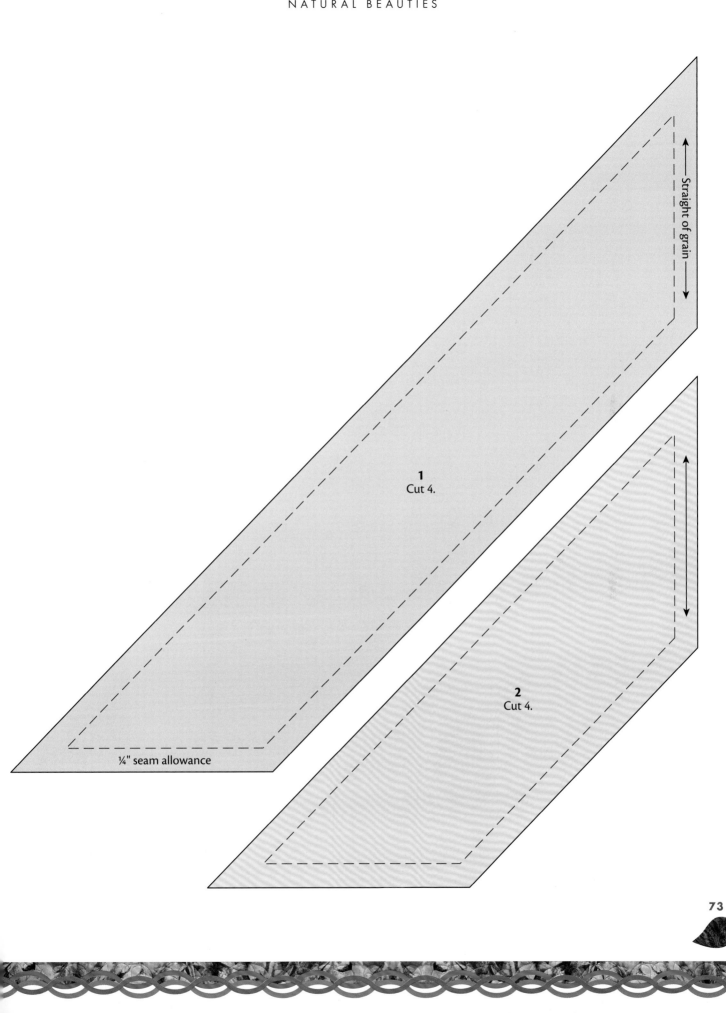

1
Cut 4.

Straight of grain

¼" seam allowance

2
Cut 4.

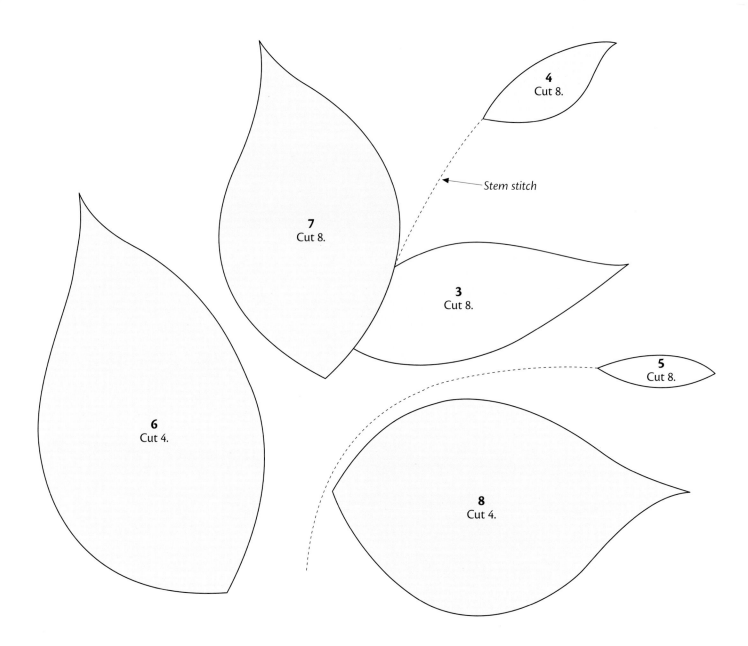

4
Cut 8.

← *Stem stitch*

7
Cut 8.

3
Cut 8.

5
Cut 8.

6
Cut 4.

8
Cut 4.

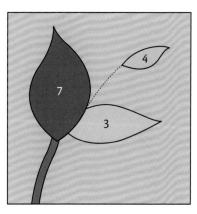

Corner block appliqué placement

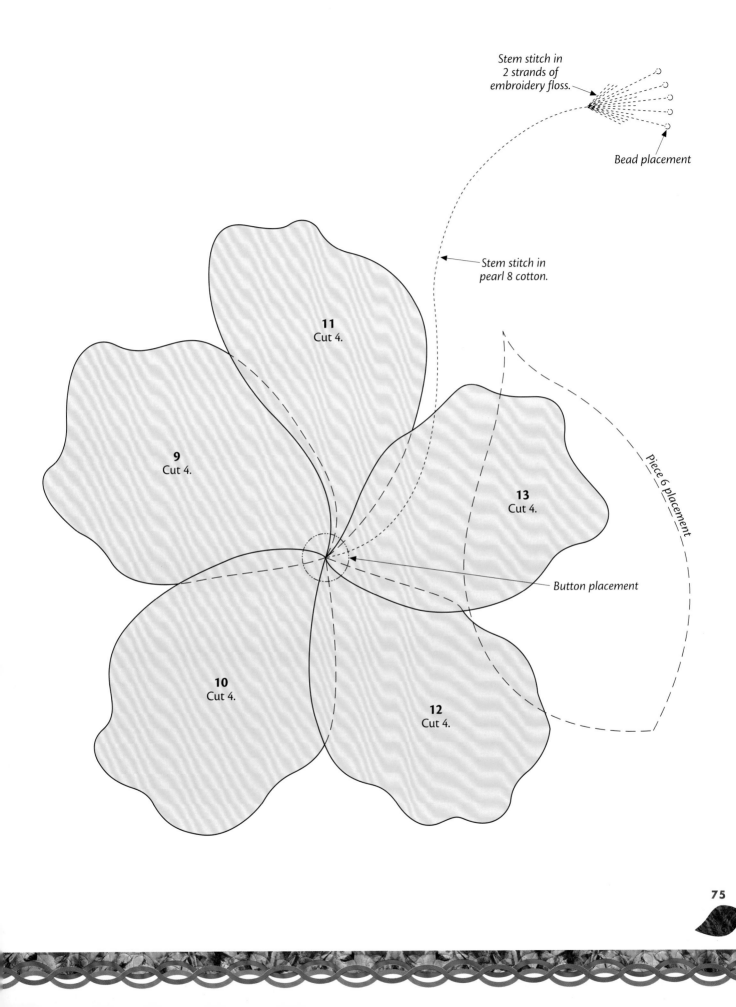

Stem stitch in 2 strands of embroidery floss.

Bead placement

Stem stitch in pearl 8 cotton.

11
Cut 4.

9
Cut 4.

13
Cut 4.

Piece 6 placement

Button placement

10
Cut 4.

12
Cut 4.

REFLECTIONS

The sea brings us gifts and leaves them tangled in the seaweed on the shore...
shells, sea glass, pebbles, and more.

MATERIALS

Yardage is based on 42"-wide fabric.

1 yard of multicolored batik for center sashings and binding

⅝ yard of green batik for center blocks and border blocks

½ yard *each* of 3 purple batiks for center blocks and appliqués

½ yard of tan batik for center blocks

¼ yard *each* of 3 green batiks for border blocks

¼ yard *each* of 2 brown batiks for center blocks

¼ yard of light brown batik for border sashings

3¼ yards of fabric for backing

58" x 58" piece of batting

1 skein (or the equivalent of 78 yards) of variegated, textured yarn for embellishment

1 skein of 6-strand embroidery floss in a color to match the yarn

24 green sparkly buttons, ⅞" diameter, for flower centers

12 brass charms for star centers

Small iron-on crystals for flower petal points

Miscellaneous sea-inspired embellishments for center swags

CUTTING

All measurements include ¼-wide" seam allowances. Refer to "Making the Blocks" (step 6) on page 78 before cutting the appliqué pieces.

From the multicolored batik, cut:
12 strips, 1½" x 8½"
12 strips, 3½" x 8½"
2 strips, 2½" x 36½"
5 strips, 2" x 42"

From *each* of the 2 brown batiks, cut:
24 of template 1 (48 total)

From the green batik, cut:
6 squares, 6½" x 6½"
48 of template 1

From *each* of the 3 green batiks, cut:
6 squares, 6½" x 6½" (18 total)

From *each* of the 3 purple batiks, cut:
4 squares, 5¼" x 5¼" (12 total); cut twice diagonally to make 16 quarter-square triangles (48 total)
8 of template 2 (24 total)

From the tan batik, cut:
48 squares, 2⅞" x 2⅞"; cut once diagonally to make 96 half-square triangles

From the light brown batik, cut:
24 rectangles, 1½" x 6½"

Quilt size: 48" x 48" ❀ Center block size: 8" x 8" ❀ Border block size: 6" x 6"

MAKING THE BLOCKS

1. Sew a tan batik half-square triangle to each side of a purple batik quarter-square triangle as shown to make a flying-geese unit. Press the seam allowances toward the tan triangles. Make four flying-geese units.

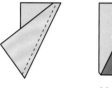

Make 4.

2. Sew a brown batik template 1 piece to a green batik template 1 piece, matching the trimmed corners as shown. For easier matching of the sharp angles, mark the seam intersections with a pencil. Insert a pin through both pieces to align them for sewing. Press the seam allowances toward the brown batik. Make four.

Make 4.

3. Sew the units from steps 1 and 2 together as shown. Press the seam allowances.

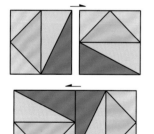

4. Repeat steps 1–3 to make a total of 12 blocks.

5. Sew one multicolored batik 1½" x 8½" strip and one multicolored batik 3½" x 8½" strip to the sides of each block. Press the seam allowances toward the sashing strips. Make 12 units.

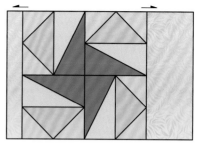

Make 12.

6. Choose your favorite appliqué method and make appliqué templates for the flowers by tracing the pattern on page 81. Refer to "Introduction to Appliqué" on page 119 for details as needed. Cut out the number of each shape indicated on the cutting list.

7. Appliqué flowers to the green batik 6½" squares.

8. Iron crystals to each of the flower petal points if desired.

ASSEMBLING THE QUILT

1. Sew four horizontal rows of three pieced blocks each, alternating the position of the blocks as shown in the quilt layout. Press the seam allowances in opposite directions.

2. Sew the two multicolored batik 2½" x 36½" strips to the top and bottom of the rows.

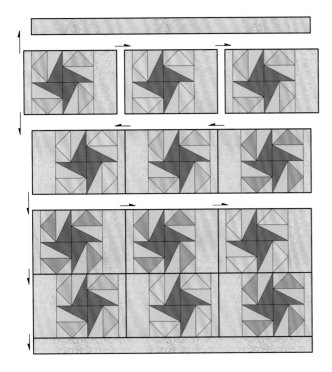

3. Construct the top and bottom border strips by sewing five green appliquéd blocks and six light brown batik 1½" x 6½" sashing strips together. Press the seam allowances toward the brown sashing strips.

4. Sew the strips to the top and bottom of the quilt. Press the seam allowances toward the border strips.

5. Construct the side border strips by sewing seven green appliqué blocks and six light brown batik 1½" x 6½" sashing strips together; press.

6. Sew the strips to the sides of the quilt; press.

FINISHING THE QUILT

Refer to "Quiltmaking Basics" on page 111 for more details as needed.

1. Mark the quilting design on the quilt top if desired. See the quilting suggestion below.

2. Layer the quilt top with batting and backing; baste or pin.

3. Quilt by hand or by machine.

4. Use the multicolored batik 2" x 42" strips to bind the edges of the quilt.

5. Add a label to the back of your quilt.

EMBELLISHING THE QUILT

1. Sew the 12 brass charms to the center of each star.

2. Sew the 24 sparkly green ⅞" buttons to the flower centers.

3. From the variegated and textured yarn, cut 2-yard lengths and divide the strands into two bundles (19 to 20 lengths in each). Tie a piece of yarn in the center of each bundle and fold in half. Separate the strands into three sections and braid, leaving a tail. Tie off the end of the tail with yarn or embroidery floss.

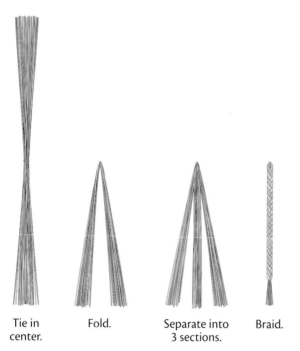

Tie in center. Fold. Separate into 3 sections. Braid.

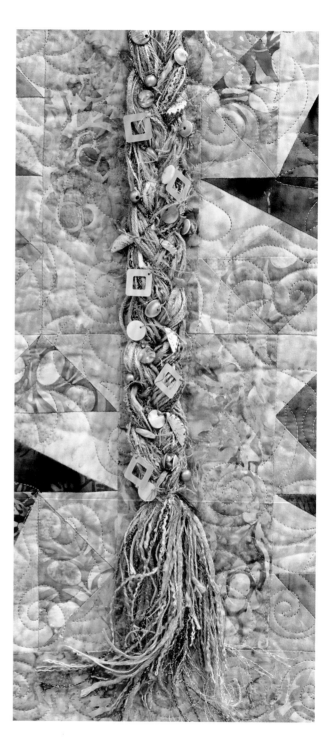

4. Attach the two braids to the center of the quilt using the matching 6-strand embroidery floss. Trim the ends to the desired length. Tie sea-inspired embellishments to the braids with two strands of the embroidery floss.

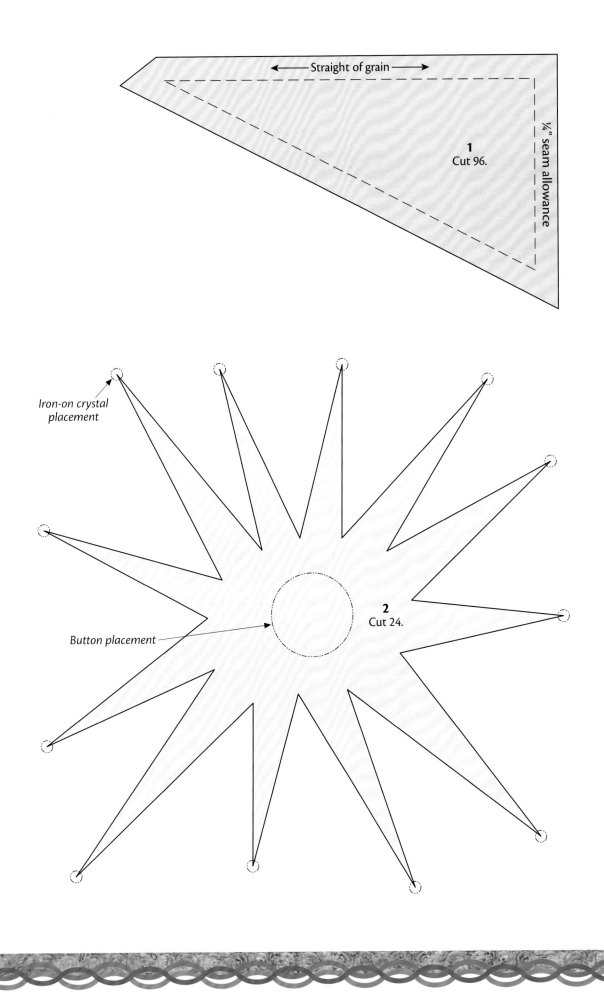

Straight of grain

¼" seam allowance

1
Cut 96.

Iron-on crystal
placement

Button placement

2
Cut 24.

TEQUILA SUNRISE

*The sun rises in all its glory, and the sparkly, embroidered
netting produces a dazzling effect.*

MATERIALS

Yardage is based on 42"-wide fabric.

1½ yards of yellow-and-orange batik for border and
binding

8 batiks ranging from dark pink and orange to light
yellow for blocks:*

⅜ yard of fabric 1 (dark pink and orange)

⅝ yard each of fabrics 2–7

¼ yard of fabric 8 (light yellow)

60" x 60" piece of netting with beading and sequin
embellishments**

3½ yards of fabric for backing

61" x 61" piece of batting

*Fabric 1 should be the darkest color and fabric 8 the
lightest color.*

**Look for netting at fabric stores that carry
dressmaking materials for proms, weddings, and
similar occasions.*

CUTTING

*All measurements include ¼" seam allowances. Cut the
fabrics by rows and keep the fabrics together for each
row until you are ready to sew the blocks. Refer to the
color guide on page 84. The colors in this quilt radiate
up from the darkest at the bottom to the lightest at the
top. Fabric 1, the darkest, is at the bottom; fabric 8, the
lightest is at the top. Each row uses two colors of fabric.*

Row 1
From fabric 1, cut:
  28 rectangles, 2½" x 4½"
From fabric 2, cut:
  35 squares, 2½" x 2½"

Row 2
From fabric 2, cut:
  28 rectangles, 2½" x 4½"
From fabric 3, cut:
  35 squares, 2½" x 2½"

Row 3
From fabric 3, cut:
  28 rectangles, 2½" x 4½"
From fabric 4, cut:
  35 squares, 2½" x 2½"

Quilt size: 51" x 51" ❀ Block size: 6" x 6"

Row 4

From fabric 4, cut:
   28 rectangles, 2½" x 4½"

From fabric 5, cut:
   35 squares, 2½" x 2½"

Row 5

From fabric 5, cut:
   28 rectangles, 2½" x 4½"

From fabric 6, cut:
   35 squares, 2½" x 2½"

Row 6

From fabric 6, cut:
   28 rectangles, 2½" x 4½"

From fabric 7, cut:
   35 squares, 2½" x 2½"

Row 7

From fabric 7, cut:
   28 rectangles, 2½" x 4½"

From fabric 8, cut:
   35 squares, 2½" x 2½"

From the yellow-and-orange batik, cut on the _lengthwise_ grain:

2 strips, 5" x 42½"

2 strips, 5" x 51½"

6 binding strips, 2" x 54"

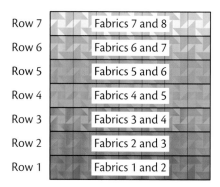

Row 7	Fabrics 7 and 8
Row 6	Fabrics 6 and 7
Row 5	Fabrics 5 and 6
Row 4	Fabrics 4 and 5
Row 3	Fabrics 3 and 4
Row 2	Fabrics 2 and 3
Row 1	Fabrics 1 and 2

Color guide

ASSEMBLING THE QUILT

1. Begin with row 1. Place a 2½" square of fabric 2 and a 2½" x 4½" rectangle of fabric 1 right sides together. Draw a diagonal line from corner to corner as shown. Stitch on the drawn line. Trim the seam allowance to ¼". Flip the triangle to the right side and press. Make four for each block, for a total of 28 for row 1.

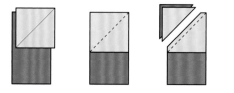

Make 28.

2. To construct the blocks, you will need to sew a partial seam. Sew one unit from step 1 to the 2½" center square of fabric 2, beginning in the middle of the square. Working in a clockwise direction, add a second unit from step 1. Add the remaining two units from step 1, and then complete the first partially sewn seam. Press the seam allowances toward the pieced rectangles. Make seven blocks for row 1.

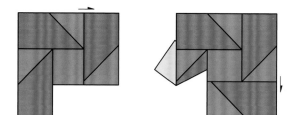

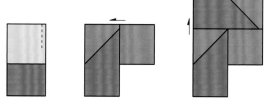

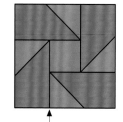

Make 7.

Finish partial seam.

3. Repeat steps 1 and 2 for each of the remaining six rows. Make a total of 49 blocks.

4. Sew the 49 center blocks into seven rows of seven blocks each. Press the seam allowances in opposite directions from row to row. Sew the rows together.

5. Sew the 5" x 42½" yellow-and-orange batik strips to the top and bottom of the quilt. Press the seam allowances toward the border strips.

6. Sew the 5" x 51½" yellow-and-orange batik strips to the sides of the quilt. Press.

FINISHING THE QUILT

Refer to "Quiltmaking Basics" on page 111 for more details if needed.

1. Layer the quilt top with the embellished netting fabric, batting, and backing; pin.

2. With the additional layer of netting, you may find it easiest to quilt by machine. See the quilting suggestion below. Make sure the quilting stitches are close enough together to hold the netting fabric securely in place.

3. Use the 2" x 54" yellow-and-orange batik strips to bind the edges of the quilt.

4. Add a label to the back of your quilt.

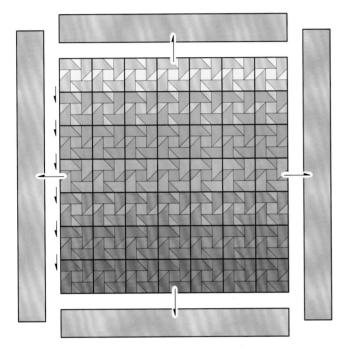

FOR THE BIRDS

Bright and happy, the jungle birds sing their joyful song.

MATERIALS

Yardage is based on 42"-wide fabric.

1⅝ yards of multicolored zigzag print for border 3

1½ yards of multicolored circle print for sashings and border 1

1½ yards of yellow print 1 for appliqués and border 2

1⅛ yards of multicolored tropical print for border 4 and binding

⅔ yard of blue-and-purple polka-dot print for appliqués and border 4

½ yard of green print 1 for background of appliqué blocks

⅓ yard of blue print for appliqués and border 4

⅓ yard of black print for bias vines

¼ yard of green print 2 for leaves

¼ yard of yellow print 2 for appliqués

⅛ yard of orange print 1 for appliqués

6" x 14" piece of black-and-blue print for bird appliqué

3" x 7" piece *each* of 3 purple prints for appliqués

Scraps of 1 pink print, 1 blue green polka-dot print, and 1 orange print 2 for appliqués

2⅔ yards of fabric for backing

46" x 76" piece of batting

3 black buttons, ½" diameter; 2 orange buttons, ¾" diameter; 1 yellow button, ¾" diameter; 4 orange buttons, ⅝" diameter; and 2 yellow buttons, ⅝" diameter for flower centers and eyes

1 skein of black 6-strand embroidery floss

CUTTING

All measurements include ¼" seam allowances.

From the green print 1, cut:
3 squares, 12½" x 12½"

From the multicolored circle print, cut on the *lengthwise* grain:
4 strips, 3½" x 12½"
2 strips, 3½" x 48½"

From the yellow print 1, cut on the *lengthwise* grain:
2 strips, 1½" x 18½"
2 strips, 1½" x 50½"

From the multicolored zigzag print, cut on the *lengthwise* grain:
2 strips, 2½" x 20½"
2 strips, 2½" x 54½"

Quilt size: 36" x 66" ✿ Appliquéd block size: 12" x 12" ✿ Pieced block size: 6" x 6"

From the multicolored tropical print, cut:

9 strips, 2½" x 42"; cut into:

  30 rectangles, 2½" x 6½"

  30 rectangles, 2½" x 4½"

6 strips, 2" x 42"

From the blue-and-purple polka-dot print, cut:

6 strips, 2½" x 42"; cut into:

  30 rectangles, 2½" x 4½"

  30 squares, 2½" x 2½"

From the blue print, cut:

2 strips, 2½" x 42"; cut into 30 squares, 2½" x 2½"

APPLIQUÉ CUTTING KEY

Refer to "Appliquéing the Quilt Center" (steps 1 and 2) before cutting the appliqué pieces.

From the black print for bias vines, cut:

½"-wide bias strips to total 75"

From the green print 2, cut:

2 *each* of templates 1–6

1 *each* of templates 1–6 reversed

From the purple print 1, cut:

1 of template 7

From the pink print, cut:

1 of template 7

From the orange print 2, cut:

1 of template 7 reversed

From the blue-and-purple polka-dot print, cut:

1 of template 8

From the blue print, cut:

1 of template 8 reversed

From the black-and-blue print, cut:

1 of template 8

From the purple print 2, cut:

1 of template 9

From the purple print 3, cut:

1 of template 9

From the blue green polka-dot print, cut:

1 of template 9 reversed

From the orange print 1, cut:

2 of template 10 and 1 of template 10 reversed

1 *each* of templates 12–18 reversed

2 *each* of templates 19–23 reversed

From the yellow print 1, cut:

2 of template 11 and 1 of template 11 reversed

From the yellow print 2, cut:

2 *each* of templates 12–18

4 *each* of templates 19–23

APPLIQUÉING THE QUILT CENTER

1. Refer to "Making Bias Stems and Vines" on page 123 to make ¼"-wide bias strips from the black print ½"-wide bias strips.

2. Choose your favorite appliqué method and make appliqué templates for the leaves, birds, and flowers by tracing the patterns on pages 91–93. Refer to "Introduction to Appliqué" on page 119 for details as needed. Cut out the number of each shape indicated in the "Appliqué Cutting Key."

3. Appliqué bias vines, leaves, and birds in position onto the green print 1 squares. Refer to the placement diagram below. Make two blocks with the birds facing right and one block reversed with the bird facing left.

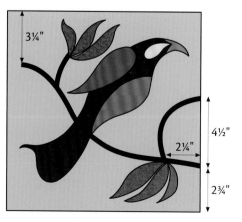

3¼"

4½"

2¼"

2¾"

Appliqué placement

4. Assemble the quilt center by alternating the multicolored circle print 3½" x 12½" strips and the three appliqué blocks in a vertical row. Press the seam allowances toward the sashing strips.

5. Sew the multicolored circle print 3½" x 48½" strips to the sides of the quilt; press.

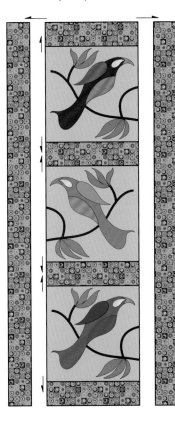

6. Appliqué all flowers in position. Embroider the birds' feet and the flower stems using a stem stitch and two strands of embroidery floss, referring to "Embroidery Stitches" on page 120.

ASSEMBLING THE QUILT

1. To add border 2, sew the yellow print 1½" x 18½" strips to the top and bottom of the quilt. Press the seam allowances toward the sashing strips.

2. Sew the yellow print 1½" x 50½" strips to the sides of the quilt; press.

3. To add border 3, sew the zigzag print 2½" x 20½" strips to the top and bottom of the quilt. Press the seam allowances toward the zigzag strips. Add the zigzag print 2½" x 54½" strips to the sides; press.

4. To piece the blocks for border 4, begin with a blue print 2½" square and a blue-and-purple polka-dot print 2½" square. Sew them together and press the seam allowance toward the polka-dot print.

5. Add a blue-and-purple polka-dot print 2½" x 4½" rectangle to the unit from step 4 and press the seam allowance toward the rectangle.

6. Add the multicolored tropical print 2½" x 4½" rectangle and then the multicolored tropical print 2½" x 6½" rectangle as shown. Make 30 blocks.

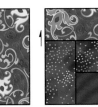 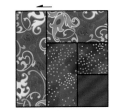

Make 30.

7. Sew two rows of four blocks each for the top and bottom borders. Position the blocks so that the last tropical print rectangle added will be on the outer edge of the quilt. Sew two rows of 11 blocks each for the side borders. Press the seam allowances all in one direction.

8. Sew the rows of four blocks each to the top and bottom of the quilt. Press the seam allowances toward the border strip.

9. Sew the rows of 11 blocks each to the sides of the quilt and press the seam allowances outward.

FINISHING THE QUILT

Refer to "Quiltmaking Basics" on page 111 for more details if needed.

1. Mark the quilting design on the quilt top if desired. See the quilting suggestion below.

2. Layer the quilt top with batting and backing; baste and pin.

3. Quilt by hand or by machine.

4. Use the multicolored tropical print 2" x 42" strips to bind the edges of the quilt.

5. Add a label to the back of your quilt.

6. Attach buttons for the flower centers and the birds' eyes.

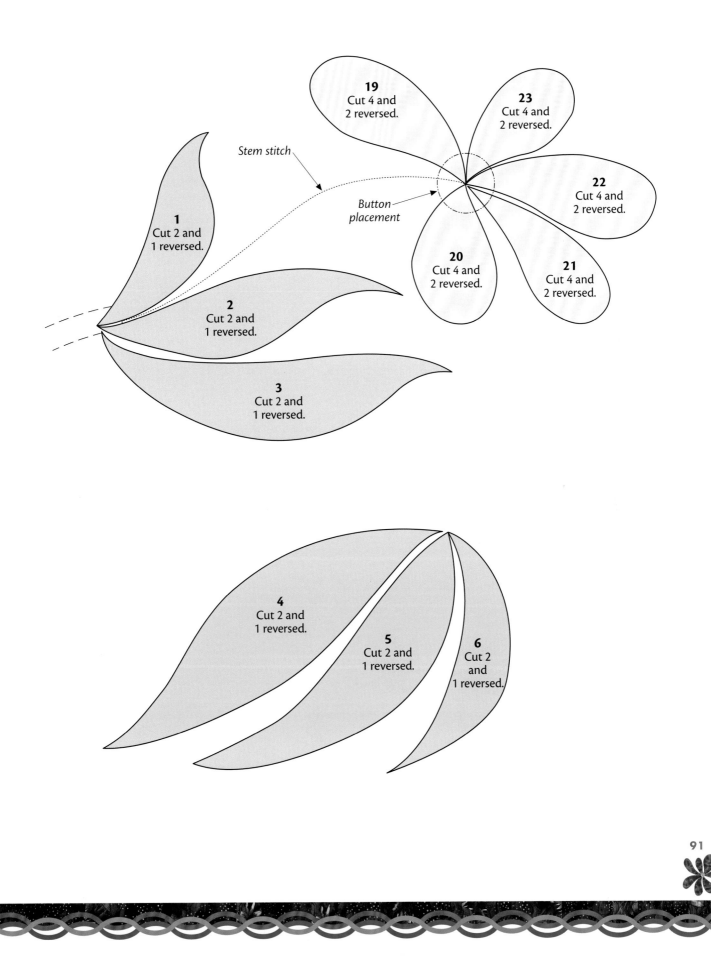

19
Cut 4 and
2 reversed.

23
Cut 4 and
2 reversed.

Stem stitch

22
Cut 4 and
2 reversed.

1
Cut 2 and
1 reversed.

*Button
placement*

2
Cut 2 and
1 reversed.

20
Cut 4 and
2 reversed.

21
Cut 4 and
2 reversed.

3
Cut 2 and
1 reversed.

4
Cut 2 and
1 reversed.

5
Cut 2 and
1 reversed.

6
Cut 2
and
1 reversed.

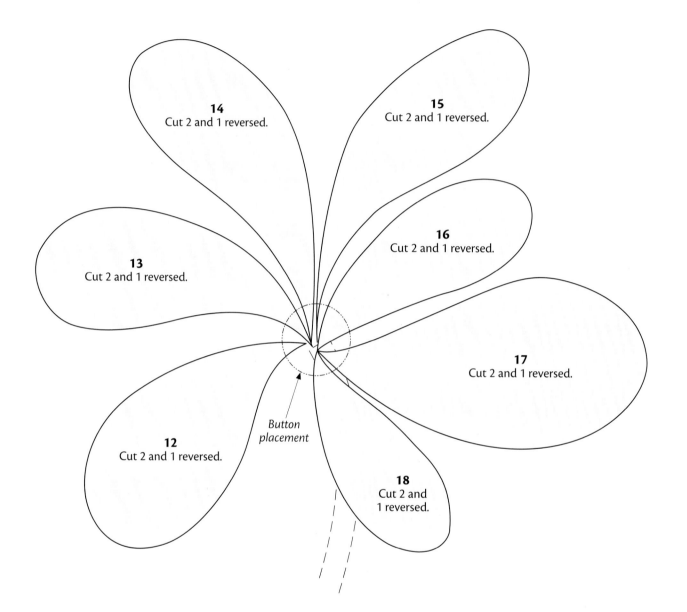

14
Cut 2 and 1 reversed.

15
Cut 2 and 1 reversed.

13
Cut 2 and 1 reversed.

16
Cut 2 and 1 reversed.

17
Cut 2 and 1 reversed.

12
Cut 2 and 1 reversed.

Button placement

18
Cut 2 and
1 reversed.

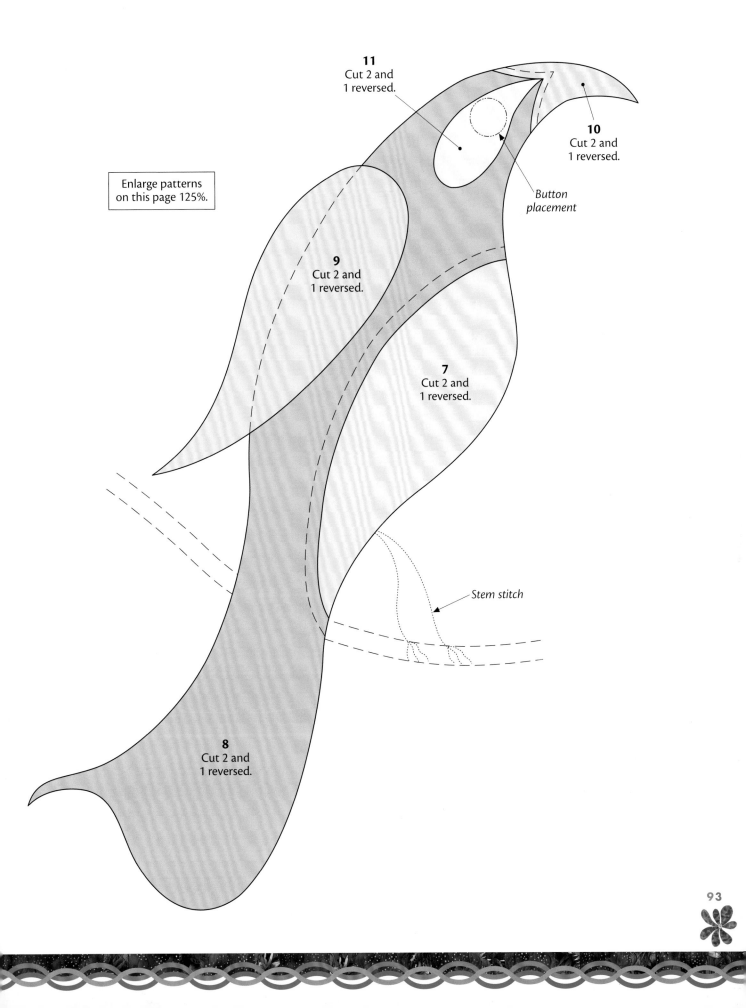

11
Cut 2 and
1 reversed.

10
Cut 2 and
1 reversed.

*Button
placement*

Enlarge patterns
on this page 125%.

9
Cut 2 and
1 reversed.

7
Cut 2 and
1 reversed.

Stem stitch

8
Cut 2 and
1 reversed.

93

PEACHY KEEN

Like a kaleidoscope, these flowers open to reveal their treasure.

MATERIALS

Yardage is based on 42"-wide fabric.

2¼ yards of deep gold tropical print for sashings and border 2

1⅔ yards of light gold print for border 1

1⅓ yards of peach polka-dot print for appliqué and border 2

1⅛ yards of pale gold print for background of blocks

½ yard of medium gold print for block borders

½ yard of medium green print 1 for appliqué and border 2

½ yard of medium green print 2 for appliqué and border 2

½ yard of medium green print 3 for appliqué and border 2

½ yard of light green print for appliqué and border 2

⅜ yard of medium peach fabric for appliqué and border 2

⅜ yard of light peach fabric for appliqué and border 2

¼ yard of dark green print for appliqué and bias stems

½ yard of rust hand-dyed fabric for binding

4½ yards of fabric for backing

77" x 77" piece of batting

16 off-white buttons of various sizes for flower centers

CUTTING

All measurements include ¼" seam allowance. Refer to "Assembling the Quilt" (step 1) on page 96 before cutting the appliqué pieces.

From the pale gold print, cut:
16 squares, 8½" x 8½"

From the peach polka-dot print, cut:
40 squares, 2" x 2"

16 of template 1

4 of template 6 and 4 of template 6 reversed

From the medium peach fabric, cut:
20 squares, 2" x 2"

16 of template 2

From the light peach fabric, cut:
20 squares, 2" x 2"

16 of template 2 reversed

Quilt size: 66" x 66" ❀ Appliqué block size: 16" x 16" ❀ Pieced block size: 6" x 6"

From the dark green print, cut:

4 *each* of templates 3 and 4

½"-wide bias strips to total 96"

From the medium green print 1:

20 squares, 2" x 2"

3 *each* of templates 3 and 4

2 of template 5

From the medium green print 2, cut:

20 squares, 2" x 2"

3 each of templates 3 and 4

2 of template 5

From the medium green print 3, cut:

20 squares, 2" x 2"

3 *each* of templates 3 and 4

2 of template 5 reversed

From the light green print, cut:

20 squares, 2" x 2"

3 *each* of templates 3 and 4

2 of template 5 reversed

From the medium gold print, cut:

8 strips, 1½" x 16½"

8 strips, 1½" x 18½"

From the deep gold tropical print, cut on the *lengthwise* grain:

2 strips, 2½" x 42½"

2 strips, 2½" x 18½"

3 strips, 2½" x 38½"

160 squares, 3½" x 3½"

From the light gold print, cut on the *lengthwise* grain:

2 strips, 6½" x 42½"

2 strips, 6½" x 54½"

From the rust hand-dyed fabric, cut:

7 strips, 2" x 42"

ASSEMBLING THE QUILT

1. Choose your favorite method of appliqué and make appliqué templates for the flowers and leaves by tracing the patterns on pages 99–101. Refer to "Introduction to Appliqué" on page 119 for details as needed. Cut out the number of each shape indicated on the cutting list.

2. Appliqué all flowers and leaves to the pale gold print 8½" squares, referring to the pattern on page 99 for placement guidance as needed.

3. Sew four appliquéd squares together to form one center block. Press the seam allowances in opposite directions. Construct four center blocks.

Make 4.

4. Sew medium gold print 1½" x 16½" strips to the top and bottom of each center block. Press the seam allowances toward the gold print strips.

5. Sew medium gold print 1½" x 18½" strips to the sides of each center block; press.

Make 4.

6. Sew two center blocks and one deep gold tropical print 2½" x 18½" strip together to make a row. Press the seam allowances toward the tropical print strip. Make two rows.

7. Sew the two center rows together, alternating them with the three deep gold tropical print 2½" x 38½" strips to form the center of the quilt; press.

8. Sew a deep gold tropical print 2½" x 42½" strip to each side of the quilt; press.

9. Refer to "Making Bias Stems and Vines" on page 123 to make ¼"-wide bias strips from the dark green print ½"-wide bias strips.

10. Fold the four light gold print 6½"-wide border strips in half to find the center; position and appliqué the flowers approximately 3" from the center of the border strips. Appliqué the bias stems to the strips. Refer to the quilt photo on page 95 for placement guidance. Wait until the borders are sewn to the quilt to appliqué the leaves.

11. Sew the two light gold print 6½" x 42½" strips to the top and bottom of the quilt. Press the seam allowances toward the border strips.

12. Sew the two light gold print 6½" x 54½" strips to the sides of the quilt; press.

13. Appliqué the leaves to all of the gold print borders.

14. To construct the pieced blocks for border 2, place any one of the 2" squares on the corner of a deep gold tropical print 3½" square right sides together, aligning raw edges. Draw a diagonal line from corner to corner as shown. Stitch on the drawn line. Trim the seam allowance to ¼". Flip the triangle to the right side and press. Repeat with all of the 2" squares to make 160 units.

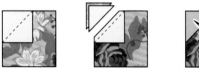

Make 160.

15. Sew four triangle units together (two with green triangles and two with peach triangles) to form one 6½" border block; press.

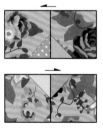 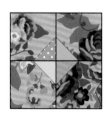

Make 40.

16. Sew nine blocks together to form a border strip. Construct two border strips. Sew them to the top and bottom of the quilt. Press the seam allowances toward the pieced border strips.

17. Sew 11 blocks together to form a side border strip. Construct two side border strips. Sew them to the sides of the quilt; press.

FINISHING THE QUILT

Refer to "Quiltmaking Basics" on page 111 for more details if needed.

1. Mark the quilting design on the quilt top if desired. See the quilting suggestion below.

2. Layer the quilt top with batting and backing; baste or pin.

3. Quilt by hand or by machine.

4. Use the rust hand-dyed 2" x 42" strips to bind the edges of the quilt.

5. Add a label to the back of your quilt.

6. Sew a cluster of four buttons in the center of each flower.

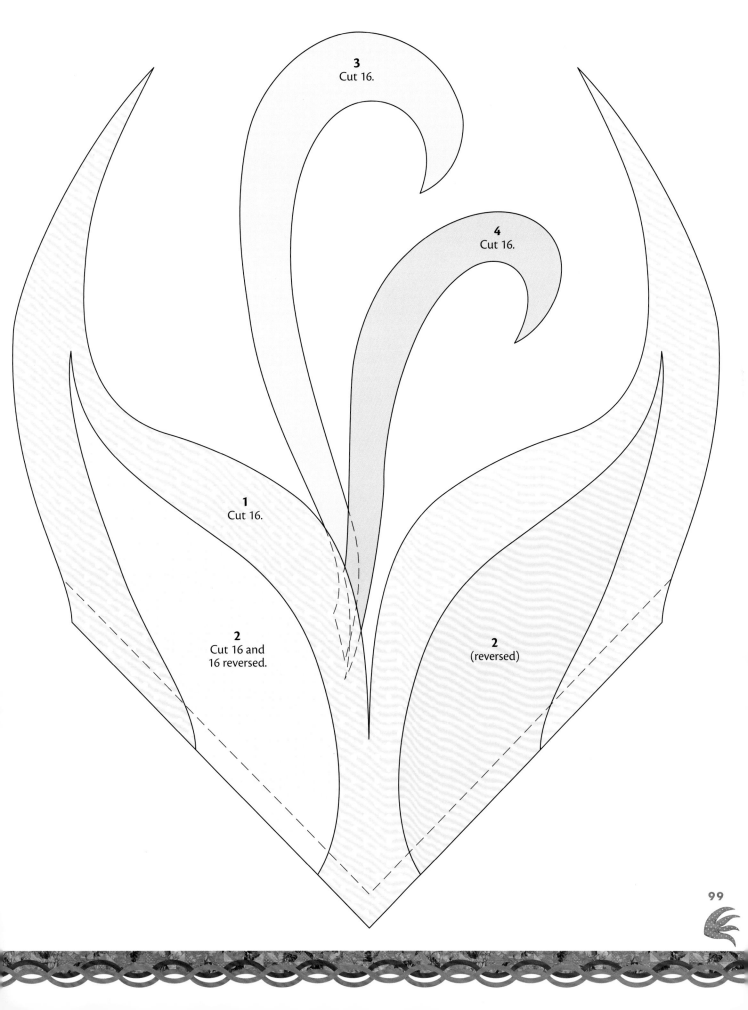

3
Cut 16.

4
Cut 16.

1
Cut 16.

2
Cut 16 and
16 reversed.

2
(reversed)

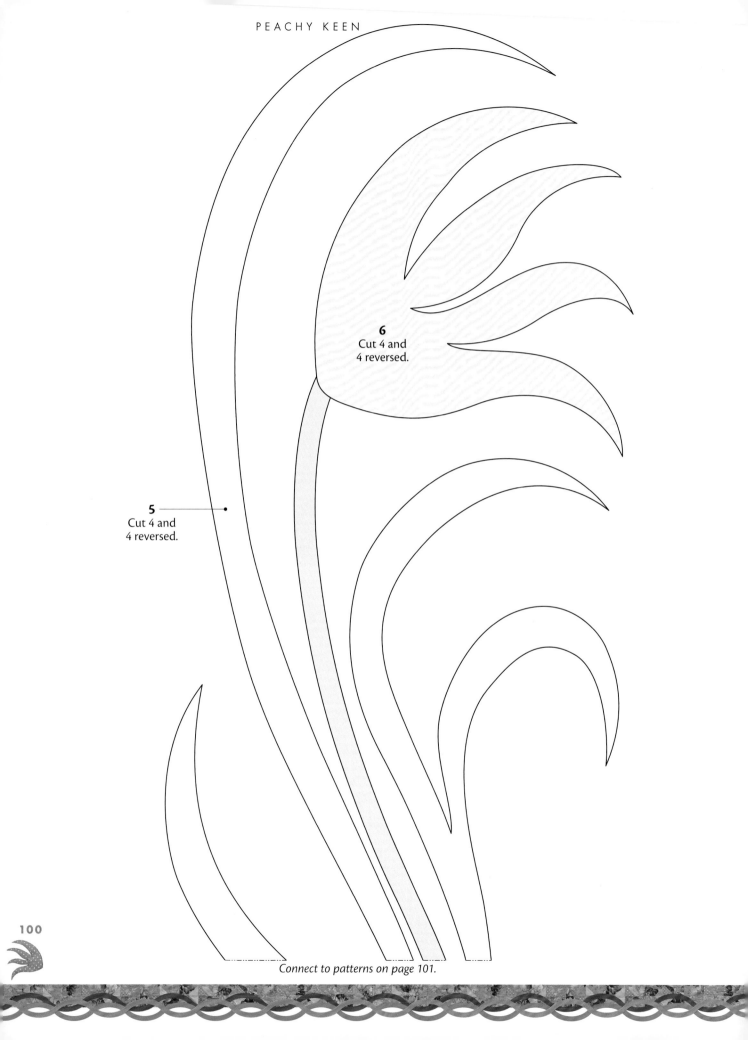

6
Cut 4 and
4 reversed.

5
Cut 4 and
4 reversed.

Connect to patterns on page 101.

Connect to patterns on page 100.

ISLAND TOTE

This fashionable bag will carry your things to the beach.
Or, take it to the market and fill it with tropical delights!

MATERIALS

Yardage is based on 54"-wide decorator-weight fabric.

- 1 yard of yellow tropical print for outer bag and pockets
- 1 yard of red tropical print for outer bag, pocket trim, and shoulder straps
- 1 yard of green tropical print for lining of bag and pockets
- 3½ yards of 22"-wide heavyweight fusible interfacing
- 8 buttons, 1⅛" diameter, in complementary colors
- 6" x 15" piece of cardboard or mat board (optional)

CUTTING

All measurements include ¼" seam allowances.

From the yellow tropical print, cut:
2 rectangles, 18½" x 21½"

2 squares, 10" x 10"

From the red tropical print, cut:
2 strips, 3½" x 21½"

4 strips, 5" x 35"

4 strips, 2" x 10"

From the green tropical print, cut:
2 squares, 21½" x 21½"

2 squares, 10" x 10"

From the heavyweight fusible interfacing, cut:
2 squares, 21½" x 21½"

2 strips, 1¾" x 66"

Size: 15½" x 19" x 5½"

ASSEMBLING THE BAG

1. Sew the red tropical print 3½" x 21½" strips to the top of the yellow 18½" x 21½" rectangles. Press the seam allowances toward the red strips. Make two outer panels.

2. Topstitch ¼" away from the seam on the red tropical print strip on both outer panels.

3. Iron the 21½" interfacing squares, to the wrong side of the two panels of the outer bag, following the manufacturer's instructions.

4. Place the two yellow tropical print 10" squares on top of the green tropical print 10" squares, wrong sides together, for the pocket.

5. Fold the four red print 2" x 10" strips in half lengthwise, wrong sides together, and press. Open out and fold each raw edge to the middle, wrong sides together, and press again.

6. Place the top edge of the pocket layers inside the folded red print edging strip. Stitch ⅛" from the double-folded edge. Repeat for the second pocket.

7. Pin one pocket to the right side of each outer-bag rectangle; center it 6" down from the top edge and 5¾" from each side. Refer to the bag diagram at right.

8. Place a red print edging strip on the bottom of each pocket, sandwiching the pocket layers as you did before. Stitch ⅛" from the double-folded edge through both the pocket and the outer bag.

9. To make the handle straps, trim the ends of the red print 5" x 35" strips to a 45° angle. Sew the two strips together. Press the seam allowance open. Cut the strip to a length of 66". Make 2 strips.

10. Fold in one long side of the 5" x 66" strip 1¾", wrong sides together, and press. Place one fusible interfacing 1¾" x 66" strip inside the fold and iron in position.

11. On the opposite side of the red print 5" x 66" strip, fold in ½" and press wrong sides together. Fold the strip over to the middle so that the folded edge covers the raw edge of the strip and the interfacing edge.

12. Sew along the fold through the center of the strap. Also sew ¼" from the edge along each side of the strap. Make two straps.

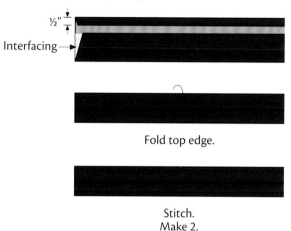

½"

Interfacing

Fold top edge.

Stitch.
Make 2.

13. Pin one strap to each side of the outer bag, covering the edges of the pocket. The outer edge of the strap will be 4¾" from the edge of the bag. Sew along the outer edges of the strap from the bottom edge up to the red trim piece. Sew two horizontal rows on the strap at the top edge of the yellow tropical print to give the shoulder straps added strength.

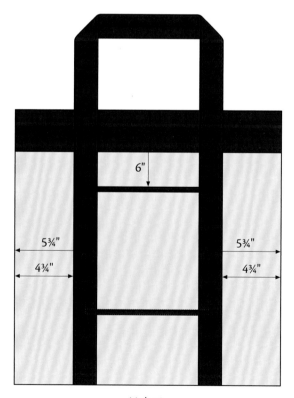

6"

5¾"   5¾"
4¾"   4¾"

Make 2.
Bag diagram

14. Place the two outer bag panels right sides together and sew using a ¼" seam allowance along the bottom and both sides. Clip the corners. Press the seam allowances open. Turn the bag right side out.

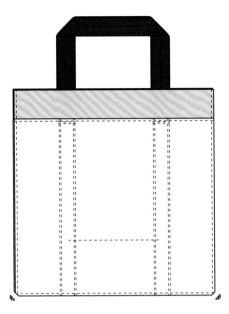

15. Place the two green tropical print 21½" squares right sides together. Sew using a ¼" seam allowance along both sides and along the bottom, leaving at least an 8" opening in the bottom seam line. Clip the corners. Press the seam allowances open.

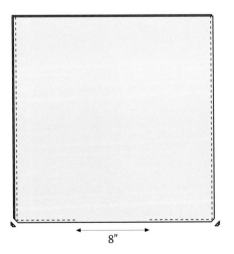

16. Place the outer bag inside the lining, right sides together. Sew using a ¼" seam allowance around the top of the bags. Make sure the handles are out of the way of the seam.

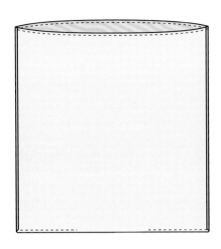

17. Pull the outer bag through the 8" opening in the bottom of the lining bag as you turn the lining right side out.

18. Close the opening in the lining bag by hand sewing the seam closed.

19. Insert the lining bag down into the outer bag. Press the top seam of the bag. Sew ¼" from the edge around the top of the bag.

20. Fold the bottom of the bag to make a triangle with 4" sides as shown, ensuring that the seam is centered. Draw a horizontal line between the two points. Sew along the line through all layers.

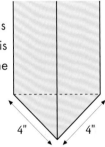

21. Tack the points to the sides of the bag with two 1⅛" buttons.

22. Sew a button at each side seam of the bag, centered in the middle of the red tropical print strip. Sew two buttons on each side of the bag between the straps. Refer to the photo on page 103 for button placement.

23. Optional: Cut a cardboard 5½" x 14½" piece to place in the bottom of the bag for additional support. You can cover it with fabric or use mat board in a complementary color.

ROMANCING
THE BAG

With lots of room to carry everything you need, this island-inspired bag will move elegantly with you from the casual sunset stroll, to the romantic dinner seaside, to star gazing late into the night.

MATERIALS

Yardage is based on 54"-wide decorator-weight fabric.

¾ yard of light green tropical print for bag, closure, and straps

½ yard of beige tropical print for lining

1 yard of 22"-wide heavyweight fusible interfacing

1 beaded napkin ring*

Look for these in import stores, bed-and-bath shops, or your favorite department store.

CUTTING

All measurements include ¼" seam allowances.

From the light green tropical print, cut:
2 each using the bag and closure pattern
2 strips, 3¼" x 24½"

From the beige tropical print, cut:
2 using the bag pattern

From the heavyweight fusible interfacing, cut:
2 using the bag pattern
2 strips, 1¼" x 24½"

ASSEMBLING THE BAG

1. Iron the fusible interfacing bag pieces to the wrong side of the two light green tropical print bag pieces, following the manufacturer's instructions.

2. Place the two light green tropical print bag pieces on top of each other, right sides together. Sew using a ¼" seam allowance around the curved edges, leaving the top open. Turn the bag right side out.

Leave open.

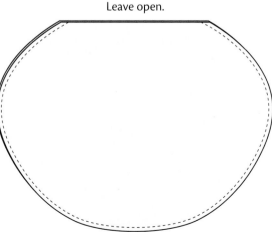

Size: 13" x 18"

3. Fold one edge of the light green tropical print 3¼" x 24½" strips over 1", wrong sides together, and press. Place a fusible interfacing 1¼" x 24½" strip inside the fold and press. Fold over ½" along the opposite side of the light green tropical print strip; press. Fold this side over the edge of the interfacing and press. Stitch along the folded edge through the center of the strap. Stitch along each edge of the strap ¼" from the edge. Make two straps.

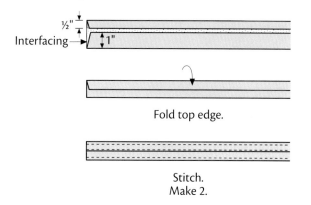

Fold top edge.

Stitch.
Make 2.

4. Position a handle on the right side of each outer bag piece; place the ends 1" away from the seam line, align the raw edges, and pin.

5. Place the two closure pieces right sides together. Stitch around the curved edges using a ¼" seam allowance; leave the straight edge open. Turn right side out and press. Topstitch ¼" around the stitched edges of the closure.

6. Pin the completed closure to the back panel of the outer bag between the handle straps.

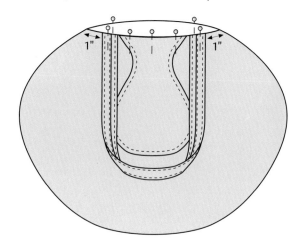

7. Place the two beige tropical print bag pieces on top of each other with right sides together. Sew using a ¼" seam allowance around the curved sides of the bag, leaving an 8" opening near the bottom.

8. Place the outer bag inside the lining bag, right sides together and sew using ¼" seam allowance around the top, catching the handles and closure in the seam.

9. Pull the outer bag through the opening in the lining bag as you turn the lining bag right side out.

10. Hand sew the opening of the lining bag closed.

11. Insert the lining bag down into the outer bag. Press the top seam of the bag. Fold the closure from the back of the bag toward the front.

12. Sew a beaded napkin ring holder to the front of the bag so the closure can easily slide through.

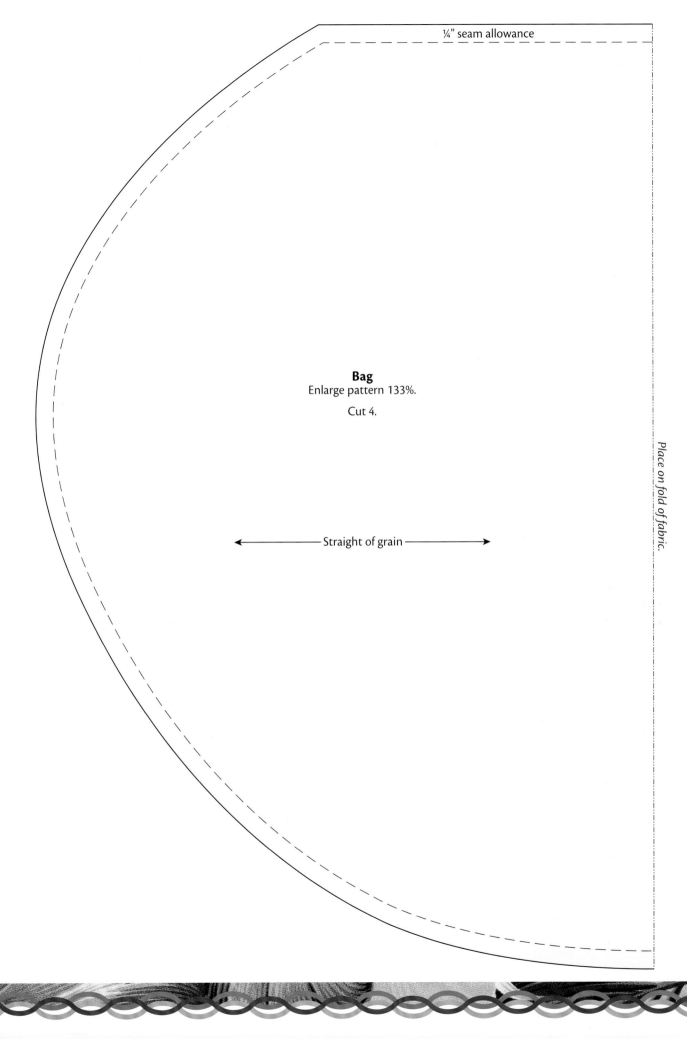

¼" seam allowance

Bag
Enlarge pattern 133%.

Cut 4.

Straight of grain

Place on fold of fabric.

¼" seam allowance

109

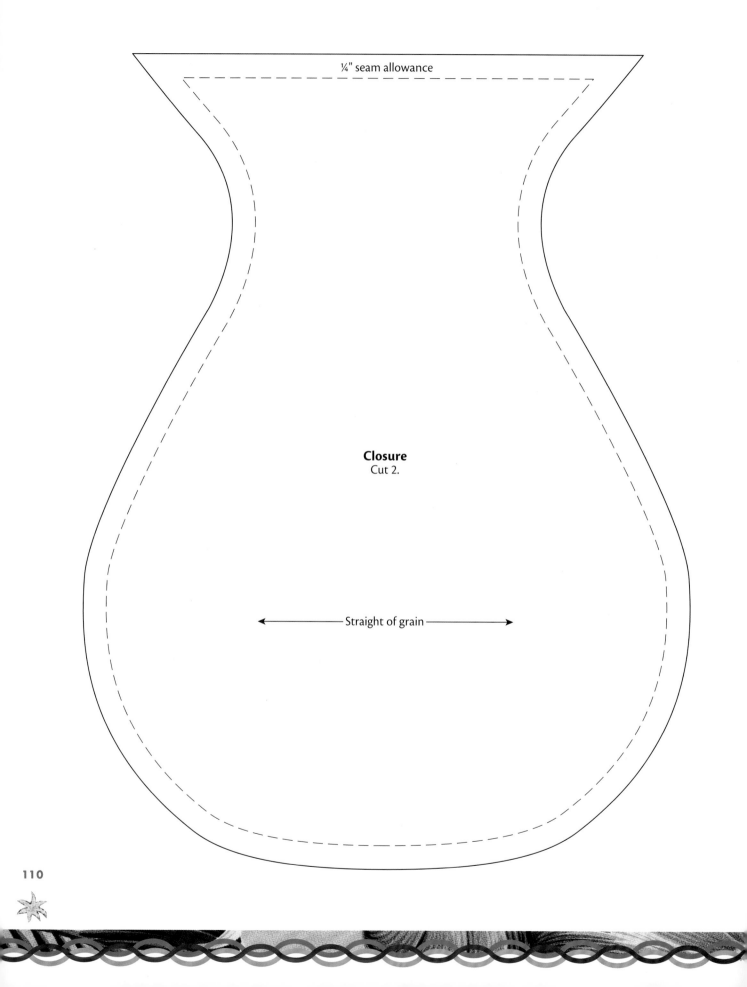

¼" seam allowance

Closure
Cut 2.

←———— Straight of grain ————→

QUILTMAKING BASICS

In this section you will find recommendations and guidelines for essential tools and techniques to enhance your quiltmaking experience.

TOOLS AND SUPPLIES

If you are a beginning quilter, purchase only the essential items you need, buying the very best quality. These tools will be an investment, and they will be part of your sewing studio for many years to come. As you expand your skills and become a more experienced quilter, it's always fun to invest in new products and try new gadgets, but you will never outgrow the basic tools.

Fabric. Purchase good-quality, 100%-cotton fabric. If you can, always purchase a little extra. Mistakes happen, and I always say, "Better a little extra, than not enough." Choose a wide variety of fabrics. It will make your quilt interesting and exciting. Always prewash, dry, and press your fabrics before you use them.

Thread. For appliqué and piecing, use good-quality cotton or cotton-covered polyester thread. For piecing, you will want to use 50-weight thread. For appliqué, you might like to use a lighter 60-weight cotton thread or a 100%-silk thread. These lighter-weight threads are easier to thread through the small eye of the thin needles (Sharps) used for appliqué.

Quilting thread comes in an array of colors and textures, in cotton, rayon, and polyester. It's fun to experiment to find just the right thread for your project.

Needles. A good-quality needle will glide through your fabric and make sewing a pleasure. Needle sizes are indicated by number: the larger the number, the smaller the needle. Choose the correct needle for each step in the quilting process.

Betweens are shorter, thicker needles used for hand quilting.

Sharps are slightly longer, thinner needles with a small eye, used for hand appliqué.

Crewels are long needles with a large eye that can accommodate heavier-weight threads that may be used to embellish your quilt.

Between ⟞━━━━━━━⟝
Sharp ⟞━━━━━━━⟝
Crewel ⟞━━━━━⟝

For machine piecing or machine quilting, use machine needles in size 70/10, 80/12, or 90/14.

Thimbles. Thimbles come in a variety of shapes, sizes, and materials. My personal favorite is an antique silver thimble given to me as a gift. It's a treasure! If you are planning to hand piece, hand appliqué, or hand quilt, wear a thimble to protect your fingertip. Try several varieties to see which is most comfortable for you.

Pins. You will need a variety of pins for various quilting tasks.

Silk pins are sharp pins with plastic or glass heads that are excellent for pinning patchwork pieces together.

Sequin pins are short, ¾" pins that are helpful for pinning appliqué pieces to the background fabric. Because of their short length, you'll be less likely to catch your sewing thread on them when doing hand appliqué.

Quilter's pins are extra-long pins with plastic heads that are used to pin the layers of the quilt together when you're planning to hand baste and hand quilt.

Safety pins are used to pin baste your quilt for machine quilting. Be sure to purchase rustproof pins.

Scissors. Use craft scissors for cutting plastic or paper templates for piecing or appliqué. Save one good-quality pair of scissors for cutting fabric only. Small, very sharp, 4" scissors are excellent for clipping threads or trimming appliqué pieces.

Seam ripper. This sharp, pointed tool makes it easy to remove small machine-stitching errors.

Marking tools. There are a variety of marking tools available to use to mark your fabric when drawing around appliqué templates, piecing templates, or drawing quilting lines. I prefer to use a No. 2 pencil or a fine-lead 0.5 mechanical pencil to lightly mark my fabric. No matter what tool you choose, be sure to test it to ensure that you can easily remove the marks.

Rotary-cutting and measuring tools. Rotary cutting is a fast, accurate way to cut your patchwork pieces. You will need a self-healing cutting mat, a rotary cutter, and some clear, acrylic rulers with both vertical and horizontal measuring lines. Some useful sizes include 4" x 4", 6" x 6", 6" x 12", 6" x 24", 8" x 14", and 15" x 15". An extra-long 120" tape measure is ideal for measuring your quilt top when adding borders.

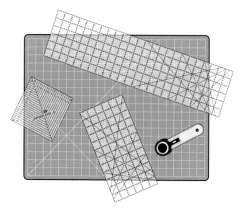

Light box. A light box usually consists of a wooden box with a plastic top and an electric light inside. They come in a variety of sizes. A light box makes it very easy to trace patterns and position your appliqué pieces on the background fabric. It is well worth the investment if you do a large amount of appliqué. If you don't have a light box, you can use a glass-topped table with a light underneath or you can tape your pattern to a window for tracing.

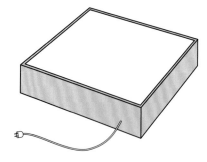

ROTARY CUTTING

Rotary cutting is usually associated with machine piecing, since the sewing line is not marked and the ¼" seam allowance is included in the cutting dimensions. Even if you are hand piecing, you can rotary cut your pieces and mark the ¼" seam allowance after cutting. It will save you from having to make templates and cut your patchwork pieces with scissors. Use a ruler and a No. 2 pencil to draw a line around the piece, ¼" inside the cut edge on the wrong side of the fabric. The drawn line will be your sewing line. See "Hand Piecing" on page 113 for additional details.

Before rotary cutting your fabric, first make a cleanup cut to straighten the edges.

1. Fold the fabric and match the selvages. Place the folded edge closest to you on the cutting mat. Align a square ruler along the folded edge of the fabric. Place a long ruler to the left of the square ruler, covering the uneven raw edges of the fabric. Remove the square ruler and hold the long ruler firmly with your left hand. Cut along the right edge of the long ruler with a rotary cutter. Now you have a straight edge to cut strips and other shapes.

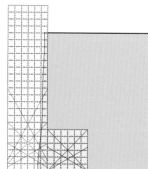
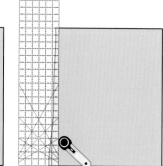

2. To cut strips, align the newly cut edge of the fabric with the line on the ruler for the required width. Cut the strip.

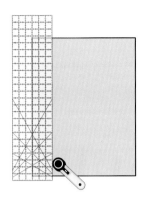

3. To cut squares or rectangles, first cut a strip the required width. Trim the ends and align the left edge with the correct ruler line. Cut the squares or rectangles as needed.

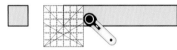

4. To cut a half-square triangle, determine the finished length of the short side of the triangle and add ⅞". Cut a square to this measurement, and cut it once diagonally. Each square yields two half-square triangles, with the straight grain of the fabric on the short sides of each triangle.

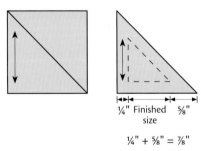

¼" Finished ⅝"
size

¼" + ⅝" = ⅞"

5. To cut a quarter-square triangle, determine the finished size of the long side of the triangle and add 1¼". Cut a square to this measurement, and then cut it twice diagonally. Each square yields

four quarter-square triangles with the straight grain of the fabric on the long side of each triangle.

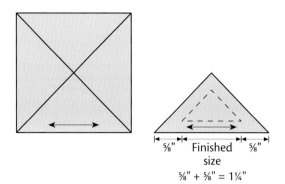

⅝" Finished ⅝"
size

⅝" + ⅝" = 1¼"

HAND PIECING

I love hand piecing because you can do it anywhere, anytime—at home or while you are traveling. Early quilts were all hand pieced, and I look upon hand piecing as the time-honored method of constructing a quilt. To cut your patchwork pieces using traditional templates and scissors, follow the steps below. To rotary cut your pieces, see "Rotary Cutting" on page 112 for details, and then begin with step 2 below.

1. Make a template from either lightweight plastic or cardboard in the exact size of the finished patchwork piece. I recommend plastic, because it will not wear down with continued use. Place the template on the wrong side of your chosen fabric, being aware of the grain lines of the fabric. Trace around the template with a No. 2 pencil. Leave at least ½" between each shape. The drawn lines are your sewing lines. Cut out each piece with scissors, leaving a ¼" seam allowance around the drawn lines.

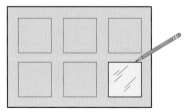

Trace around the template.

2. Place two fabric pieces right sides together and pin, matching pencil lines exactly at the corners and along the seam line. Use a regular sewing thread in a matching color, knotted at the end. Stitch the fabric pieces together using a short

running stitch. Backstitch and knot the thread at the beginning and end of each seam to secure your stitching. Seam allowances should remain free. Trim seam allowances so they are $\frac{1}{8}$" to $\frac{1}{4}$" wide. Press the seam allowances toward the darker fabric when possible. When sewing patchwork units together, avoid sewing across the seam allowances. On long seams, backstitch at regular intervals to secure your stitching.

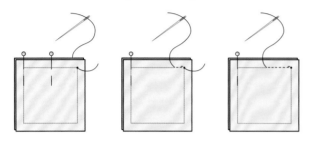

MACHINE PIECING

The most important thing to remember in machine piecing is to maintain an accurate $\frac{1}{4}$" seam allowance so that all your patchwork pieces fit together perfectly. Set your machine stitch length at approximately 10 to 12 stitches per inch. Line up the cut edges of your fabric pieces precisely and stitch. Backstitching is not necessary, because the seams will cross each other.

Chain piecing your patches saves both time and thread, and it is an especially efficient method if you are sewing several identical units. To chain piece, sew your first pair of patches together. At the end of the seam line, stop sewing but do not cut the thread. Feed the next pair of patches under the presser foot and continue sewing in the same manner until all of the patches are sewn. Remove the chain of patches from the machine and clip the threads between the pairs of sewn patches.

If you need to sew two patches or units together that are slightly different in size, pin the pieces together as they should match, distributing the fullness evenly between the pins and adding pins if necessary. Sew

the seam with the larger piece of fabric underneath. The feed dogs will ease the bottom fabric to fit with the top fabric.

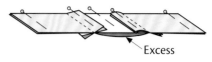

Excess

Press seam allowances as you go. Plan your pressing so that the seam allowances are pressed in opposite directions. This eliminates bulk and ensures that the seam allowances nestle together as you sew. Press seam allowances toward the darker fabric when possible.

Opposing seams

SEWING THE BLOCKS TOGETHER

For the quilts in this book, blocks are sewn together in a straight setting. Please remember to follow these basic steps:

1. Ensure that each block is the same size.

2. Sew the blocks of each row together.

3. Press the seam allowances in opposite directions from row to row.

4. Sew the rows together.

5. Press as you go.

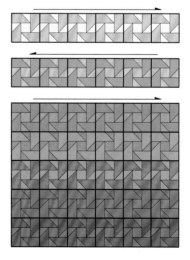

ADDING BORDERS

After you have sewn all the blocks together, it is time to add the borders. Seam allowances can vary and some stretching can occur as you handle your blocks, so always measure through the center of your quilt to determine the exact length of your borders. This will prevent your borders from rippling. In the cutting instructions, I often have you cut the border strips longer than necessary; this allows you to cut the border strips to the exact measurement of your quilt later.

borders with butted corners

1. To add the top and bottom borders, measure widthwise across the center of your quilt. Trim the top and bottom border strips to this measurement and sew them to the top and bottom of your quilt. Press the seam allowances toward the borders.

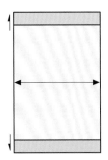

2. To add the side borders, measure lengthwise through the center of your quilt, including the top and bottom borders. Trim the side border strips to this measurement and sew them to the sides of your quilt. Press the seam allowances toward the borders.

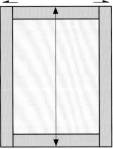

3. Repeat this process for each border added.

borders with corner blocks

1. Measure your quilt through the width and length. Cut the four border strips to these measurements.

Sew the side border strips to the quilt top. Press the seam allowances toward the borders.

2. Cut corner squares the required size. Sew a corner square to each end of the top and bottom border strips. Press the seam allowances toward the border strips. Sew the top and bottom border units to the quilt top, matching seams. Press seam allowances toward the border strips.

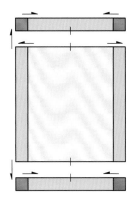

MARKING QUILTING DESIGNS

Now that the quilt top is complete, you need to decide whether you will quilt by hand or machine and what designs you will use. If you want to quilt a complex design that requires marking, it's best to mark the quilt top before layering and basting the quilt. This will ensure accurate lines that are easy to follow. You may find it easier to tape your quilt top to the floor or a large table with masking tape to keep it from slipping and make it easier to mark.

Always test any marking tool to ensure that the marking lines will be covered by the quilting stitch or easy to remove when the quilting process is complete.

To draw straight lines on your quilt, use an acrylic ruler with multiple parallel lines to keep your drawn lines straight. For more complex designs you may want to purchase quilting templates or stencils that come in a wide array of sizes and designs.

BACKING

I love to use print fabrics for the backing of my quilts. Once the quilt is quilted, it's like getting two quilts in one. Print fabrics also camouflage less-than-perfect quilting stitches.

Cut the backing fabric 5" larger than the quilt top on all sides (10" larger overall). This makes hand quilting the borders of your quilt less frustrating, because you will have enough fabric to fit into a quilting frame or hoop.

It may be necessary to piece the backing of your quilt using two lengths of fabric, and sometimes if the quilt is very large, three. You may place the seams either horizontally or vertically to make the best use of your fabric. Press the seam allowances open to eliminate bulk.

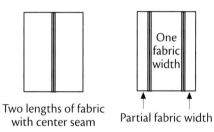

Two lengths of fabric with center seam | One fabric width | Partial fabric width

BATTING

How you plan to quilt and how you plan to use your quilt will determine the type of batting to use. You may choose from polyester, cotton, a cotton-and-polyester blend, or wool. If you are planning to hand quilt, generally the thinner the batting, the easier it is to quilt. If you are hand quilting and choose to use a cotton batting, try to avoid those that contain a bonding material called *scrim*. The scrim does help stabilize the batting, but it makes it difficult to hand sew.

Thin- to medium-weight battings in the above materials may be used for machine quilting. Thicker, heavier-weight battings are usually used only if you plan to tie your quilt.

LAYERING THE QUILT

You are now ready to baste the quilt top, batting, and backing together so that they don't shift during the quilting process. Be sure to press the backing and the top before basting so they are wrinkle free and easy to handle.

1. Place the backing right side down on a large table or the floor. Use 1½"-wide masking tape to fasten the corners and sides of the backing to the table or floor, smoothing away any ripples as you work.

2. Lay the batting on top of the backing. Smooth out any ripples. Trim the batting so it's the same size as the backing fabric.

3. Lay the quilt top right side up on top of the batting. Use masking tape to fasten the corners and sides of the quilt top in position, smoothing out any ripples as you work.

4. **For machine quilting,** use rustproof safety pins to baste the layers together. Basting stitches can easily get caught on the sewing machine as you're quilting. Place pins about 4" apart. Remove the masking tape.

   For hand quilting, pin all layers together with long quilter's pins. Hand baste all three layers together using a light-colored thread. Dark threads may stain light fabrics if left in for a long period of time. Stitch basting rows both horizontally and vertically, approximately 4" to 6" apart. Also place a row of basting around all edges of the quilt. Remove the pins and masking tape.

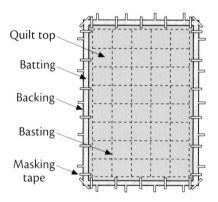

Quilt top
Batting
Backing
Basting
Masking tape

HAND QUILTING

For hand quilting, use quilting thread and a short Between needle. Beginners might do best with a larger needle, such as a size 8, until they become comfortable with the quilting process. Quilting Betweens range in size from 8 to 12; the larger the number, the smaller the needle. In hand quilting the object is to achieve small, even stitches. With practice, your stitch size and spacing will become consistent.

Most hand quilters prefer to use a hoop to support the quilt while they work. This can be a hoop held in your lap or supported on a stand.

1. Place the quilt in the hoop. Make sure the quilt is not pulled too tightly within the frame, because this can distort the quilt and make it difficult to achieve the rocking motion that produces small, even stitches.

2. Thread the needle with an 18" to 20" length of quilting thread; knot one end.

3. Approximately 1" from where you want to start quilting, insert the needle between the layers of the quilt and come up at the point where you wish to start. Tug the thread and pop the knot through the fabric so that it is buried between the layers of the quilt.

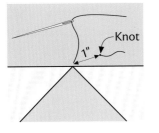

4. Wear a thimble with a raised edge on your middle finger to help control and push the needle during the rocking, up-down motion of the needle. Place your other hand under the quilt to ensure that the needle is traveling through all three layers of the quilt with each stitch. Use your thimble to push the needle down through the layers until you feel it with the fingers of your underneath hand. Then rock the needle back up through the layers to the top. Repeat to load several stitches on the needle before pulling the thread through.

5. At the end of the quilting line, take a small back-stitch. Make a knot close to the surface of the quilt top. Tug and pop the knot so that it is buried between the quilt layers. Clip the thread close to the surface of the quilt top, and the tail will disappear between the layers of the quilt.

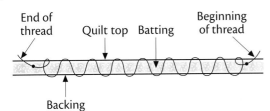

6. When the quilting is complete, remove all basting threads from the quilt.

MACHINE QUILTING

If you plan to machine quilt, you will find it helpful to have a walking foot for straight-line quilting and a darning foot for free-motion quilting. Some machines have a built-in walking foot while other machines require a separate attachment. Follow the manufacturer's recommendations for your particular sewing machine or equipment and practice until you are comfortable with the techniques.

 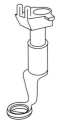

Walking foot   Darning foot

BINDING

Before binding your quilt, trim the excess batting and backing even with the quilt top and square up the corners and sides so that they are as straight and even as possible. Remove all excess threads. If you have not quilted up to the outer edges of the quilt, you may wish to baste closely along the edges of your quilt to prevent the edges from slipping while you are adding the binding.

To determine the length of binding you will need, measure all four sides of your quilt and add 18". Cut the binding strips 2" wide for a ¼"-wide finished binding.

1. Stitch the end of the strips together on the diagonal to create one long binding strip. Trim the excess fabric and press the seam allowances open to eliminate bulk. Trim the ends of the binding at a 45° angle.

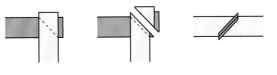

2. Fold the strip in half lengthwise, wrong sides together, and press.

3. Starting in the center on one side of the quilt, place the binding on top of the quilt with raw edges together. Start sewing several inches from the end of the binding. Sew through all layers using a ¼" seam allowance.

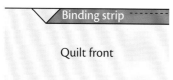

4. Stop ¼" from the corner. Cut the threads and remove the quilt from the machine. Fold the binding strip up so that the fold forms a 45° angle. Holding the 45° fold in place, bring the binding down so that all raw edges meet. Start sewing from the edge of the quilt through all layers.

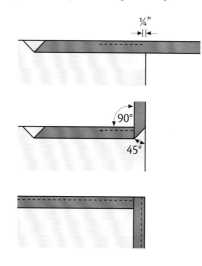

5. Continue around the quilt in the same manner. Stop sewing several inches from where you started and backstitch. Cut the threads. Remove the quilt from the machine. Lap the starting end of the binding over the tail end. Mark a diagonal line on the tail end even with the edge of the starting binding. Cut the tail end at a 45° angle, ½" past your mark.

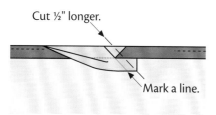

Cut ½" longer.

Mark a line.

6. Sew the two ends together with right sides facing. Press the seam allowance open. Refold the binding in half and press. Finish sewing the binding in place.

7. Turn the binding over the edge and hand stitch using a blind stitch. Make sure to cover any machine stitching. Miter each corner by folding down first one side and then the other.

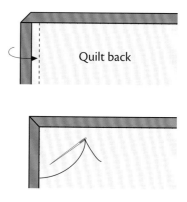

Quilt back

LABELING YOUR QUILT

You have one last important step before you are done. Years from now, future generations will admire your work and want to know more about you. Be sure to label your quilt and provide as much information as possible. Include the name of the quilt, your name, your hometown and state or country, and the date. You may also wish to include the quilt recipient's name, if the quilt is a gift, and any other relevant background information. A plain fabric such as muslin is a good choice for your label. Be sure to use waterproof marking materials to create your label. Sew the label to the back of the quilt as you would an appliqué piece.

INTRODUCTION TO APPLIQUÉ

Appliqué continues to excite me as no other area of quilting ever has. It gives you complete freedom of expression and allows you to realize your dreams and visions—visions you can touch and make reality.

Though I know many people are intimidated by the prospect of hand appliqué, the techniques are actually very easy to master with a little patience and practice.

Whether you choose fusible appliqué or traditional appliqué for your project, you can produce stunning results. Fusible appliqué lets you use all those wonderful decorative stitches and fabulous threads that are now in abundance in the market—what I call the condiments of quilting that add so much spice and texture. Traditional appliqué gives a smooth edge, adding depth and a multidimensional look to your projects. On many of my quilts, I mix both techniques to add more variety and texture.

In this book, I've included three different methods of appliqué: fusible, freezer paper, and needle turn. Each method uses slightly different techniques. As you master the techniques, you will find your favorite and use it to your best advantage. Experiment. Try them all so you have the ability to use the technique that best expresses you in your project. Remember there is no right or wrong technique among the three. It's only what works best for you.

FUSIBLE APPLIQUÉ

Fusible appliqué is fast and easy because there are no seam allowances to turn under. Instead, a bonding material called fusible web adheres the appliqué piece to the background fabric. Is fusible appliqué cheating? No, absolutely not! The web is just a helping hand to hold your appliqué piece in position until you can sew it down. In many instances, fusible appliqué is my preferred method. In fusible appliqué,

all your stitches are showcased on the top of the quilt, rather than underneath like they are in traditional appliqué. I enjoy hand stitching, and fusible appliqué allows me to use a variety of embroidery stitches in combination with embellishments, adding depth and visual interest to my quilt. If you like to use your machine, rather than hand stitch, this is an opportunity to use all those wonderful stitches on the side panel of your sewing machine to cover the edges of your motifs.

Fusible web has smooth paper on one side and an adhesive on the reverse. There are many brands on the market, including HeatnBond, Wonder Under, and Steam-A-Seam. If you're going to hand stitch your project, choose the lightest-weight fusible web possible. This is especially important if you are hand stitching through multiple layers of fused fabrics, because the adhesive stiffens the fabric. Even if you are machine stitching the edges of your motifs, you will still want your quilt to be soft and pliable. If your design results in multiple layers of fused fabrics, you can reduce the stiffness of your project by cutting away all but ¼" of the fusible web inside the traced lines before fusing it to your fabric. This trimming allows the shape to adhere to the background fabric but eliminates the stiffness of the adhesive within the shape.

Fusible web

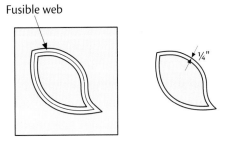

Be sure to follow the manufacturer's instructions for the fusible product you use.

"Does fusible appliqué hold up to long-term wear and tear?" is a question I am frequently asked. Yes it does! I recently hand stitched a fusible appliqué block and put it though the heavy-duty cycle of my washing machine five times. Dried and pressed, it looked fabulous!

With fusible appliqué, you will draw or trace your templates in reverse. Use a light box, if available, or an alternative arrangement for tracing. Refer to "Light Box" on page 112.

1. Place your pattern right side down on your light box. Place the fusible web on top of your pattern, with the smooth paper side up.

2. Use a pencil to trace around the appliqué pattern.

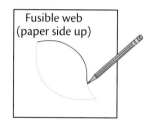

Fusible web
(paper side up)

3. Cut the shape from the fusible web, leaving approximately ¼" outside the traced lines.

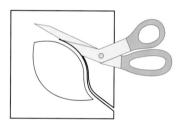

4. Place the fusible-web shape on the wrong side of your chosen fabric. Following the manufacturer's instructions, press with an iron. Let cool.

5. Before cutting out the fabric shape, pull up slightly on one corner of your fusible web to loosen it. This makes it easier to remove the paper and prevents your fabric from fraying. Now cut out the fabric shape on your drawn lines and remove the backing paper.

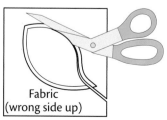

Fabric
(wrong side up)

6. Using your pattern as a guide, position the appliqué shape adhesive side down on the right side of the background fabric and press.

7. When all the pieces are fused, finish the edges with a decorative stitch, either by hand or by machine.

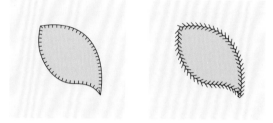

EMBROIDERY STITCHES

When I hand stitch the edges of fusible appliqué motifs, my two favorite stitches are the blanket stitch and the feather stitch. I use one strand of six-strand embroidery floss in a complementary color.

Blanket stitch: Bring the needle up in the background at the edge of the appliqué piece. Working from left to right, insert the needle down in the appliqué and bring it back up along the edge at a right angle to the edge as shown. The thread should be underneath the needle point. Continue stitching along the edge of the appliqué, keeping the stitch length consistent with the distance between stitches.

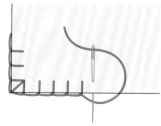

Feather stitch: Bring the needle up at A and down at B, creating a U shape. Bring the needle up at C to anchor the U shape, and then insert it down at D, creating a second U. Repeat. Keep your stitches small and ensure that the edges of the motif are covered by the stitches.

The following are additional embroidery stitches you may want to use to embellish your quilting projects.

Stem stitch: Bring the needle up at A and down at B. Repeat, bringing the needle up at C and down at D. Continue, keeping the thread on the same side of the stitching line. This is a nice stitch for tendrils and vines.

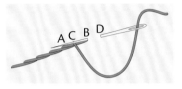

French knots: Bring the needle up at A. Wrap the thread around the needle twice (or as many times as it takes to make a knot the size you desire). Holding the thread firmly, insert the needle back down at B, as close as possible to A without going in the same hole. Hold the knot in place as the needle is pulled through to the back of the fabric. Pull tight to create the knot. A grouping of French knots makes a nice flower center.

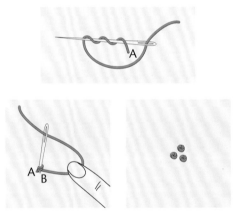

FREEZER-PAPER APPLIQUÉ

Freezer-paper appliqué has the look and feel of traditional needle-turn appliqué, but in fact, it's a much easier process. The freezer paper acts as a sewing guide, eliminating the need for drawn lines that must be hidden during the appliqué process.

Freezer paper is sold in most supermarkets in the same aisle as the plastic bags and storage containers. It is a white, heavy paper, dull on one side and shiny on the reverse. Be sure to purchase paper that is plastic coated.

In freezer-paper appliqué, you turn under a seam allowance using the freezer paper as a guide either on top or underneath the appliqué piece. I prefer to use the freezer-paper-underneath method but I encourage you to try both methods to see which method works best for you. You can reuse the templates several times, if you wish, before discarding them.

freezer paper underneath

1. Place the pattern right side down on a light box. Place the freezer paper shiny side down on top of the pattern and trace around the pattern with a pencil. As with fusible appliqué, freezer-paper templates for this method should be the reverse of the final design.

2. Cut out the freezer-paper template on the drawn lines.

3. Place the template on the wrong side of your chosen fabric; press.

4. Trim the fabric around the paper template, leaving a 1/8" to 1/4" seam allowance.

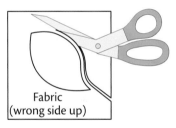

Fabric
(wrong side up)

5. Place your appliqué piece in position, paper side down, using your pattern as a guide. Pin in position with 3/4" sequin pins.

6. Thread a Sharp needle with a colored thread that matches the color of the piece you are appliqué-ing. Knot the end.

7. Turn under a small section of seam allowance using the edge of the freezer paper as a folding guide. Start your first stitch by bringing the needle up through the background fabric and through the edge of the folded appliqué fabric. Insert the needle back down through the background fabric and up again about 1/8" away.

8. Continue to take small, even stitches in a counter-clockwise direction, turning under the seam allow-

121

ance as you go and catching just the edge of the fold with each stitch.

Appliqué stitch

9. When you are about ½" from where you started stitching, fold under the remaining seam allowance and finger-press. Using tweezers, loosen the enclosed freezer paper and remove it through the unstitched opening.

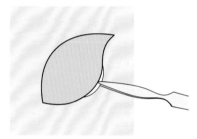

10. Refold the seam allowance and continue stitching a couple stitches past where you began. Make a knot on the wrong side of the background fabric.

freezer paper on top

1. Place your pattern right side up on the light box. Place the freezer paper shiny side down on top of the pattern and trace around the appliqué design with a pencil. Cut out the freezer-paper template on the drawn lines.

2. Place the template shiny side down on the right side of your chosen fabric; press.

3. Cut around the paper template, leaving a ⅛" to ¼" seam allowance.

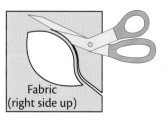

Fabric
(right side up)

4. Place your appliqué piece in position, paper side up, using your pattern as a guide. Pin in position with ¾" sequin pins.

5. Use the edge of the freezer paper as your guide for turning under the seam allowance. Stitch as described in steps 6–8 of "Freezer Paper Underneath" on page 121.

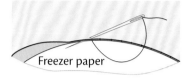

Freezer paper

6. Continue stitching a couple of stitches past where you began. Knot the thread on the wrong side of the background fabric. Remove the freezer paper.

NEEDLE-TURN APPLIQUÉ

Traditional needle-turn appliqué is the tried-and-true method our grandmothers used. It works especially well on very small or intricate appliqué pieces. The only thing you have to remember is to be sure to turn under enough seam allowance to cover your drawn lines.

1. Place your pattern right side up on a light box. Make a template of the appliqué design. Cut out the template on the drawn lines. The template material may be plastic, cardboard, or even freezer paper. If you will reuse the template several times, make it from template plastic so the piece retains the correct size and shape.

2. Place the template on the right side of the chosen appliqué fabric and trace around it with a No. 2 pencil.

3. Cut out the fabric shape, leaving a ⅛" to ¼" seam allowance.

4. Place your appliqué piece in position, right side up, using your pattern as a guide. Pin in position using ¾" sequin pins.

5. Thread a Sharp needle with a thread that matches the color of the piece you are appliquéing. Knot the end.

6. Turn under a small section of seam allowance using your needle and finger-press. Start your first stitch by bringing the needle up through the background fabric and through the edge of the folded

fabric. Insert the needle back down through the background fabric and up again about ⅛" away.

7. Continue to take small, even stitches in a counter-clockwise direction, turning under the seam allowance with the tip of the needle as you go and catching just the edge of the fold with each stitch. Be sure to turn under enough seam allowance to cover your drawn lines.

8. Continue stitching a couple of stitches past where you began. Knot the thread on the wrong side of the background fabric.

HELPFUL HINTS FOR HAND APPLIQUÉ

Whether you choose the freezer-paper or needle-turn appliqué method, the tips outlined below will help you achieve a quality finished project.

• Sew your motifs to the background fabric in the order indicated on your pattern. Remember that you are building a picture and you must work from the background out to the foreground.

• It isn't necessary to sew edges that will be covered by other motifs.

• When you turn under the seam allowance, use the tip of your needle. You may also use what I call the tooth-pick method. Use a Chinese toothpick (pointed on only one end) or a regular round toothpick. Moisten it slightly and use the point to roll, turn, and smooth the seam allowance ahead of you as you sew.

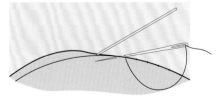

• If you are working with fabric that frays easily, leave a larger-than-normal seam allowance when cutting

around the template. Trim to the required ⅛" to ¼" as you stitch the appliqué piece in position.

• When appliquéing both inner and outer curved edges, clip the seam allowance at regular intervals to allow the seam allowance to expand and curve smoothly.

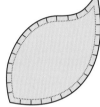

• When appliquéing an inner point, clip at the point. Stitch to the clip, take one or two stitches right at the clip, and then turn and continue to sew.

• When appliquéing an outer point, take two stitches at the point. Flip the point back and trim away excess fabric from underneath before turning and continuing to sew down the next side. This should give you a sharp, flat point.

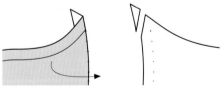

Flip back and trim excess fabric.

MAKING BIAS STEMS AND VINES

Bias strips are used for making flower stems and vines. Using a bias-tape maker is the fastest and easiest method I have found to make bias stems. This tool comes in a variety of sizes from ¼" to 2". To make a

⅛"- to ¼"-wide bias stem, cut a ½"-wide bias strip at a 45° angle to the selvage of your fabric. Use your longest rotary ruler and line up the 45° angle with the selvage edge.

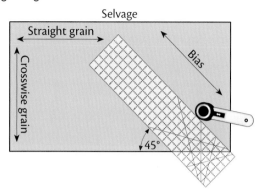

You may need to piece strips together to obtain the length needed. To do this, place the strips right sides together at a right angle, offsetting them by ¼". Stitch together using a ¼" seam allowance. Press the seam allowances open to minimize bulk.

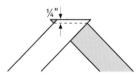

1. Place one end of the bias strip into a ¼" bias-tape maker. Pull just the tip of the strip through the bias-tape maker and pin it to your ironing board.

2. Continue to pull the bias-tape maker slowly along the strip, following close behind the bias-tape maker with your iron to crease the edges of the fabric as it emerges from the bias-tape maker. If you are working with fabric that will not hold a crease well, lightly spray the bias tape with spray starch and press.

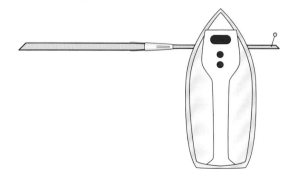

3. Pin the stem or vine in position with ¾" sequin pins; appliqué with matching thread.

EMBELLISHMENTS

Embellishments are the *condiments* of quilting. They add spice and tactile surprises, which make your quilt unique and special. It's incredible, when you look, how many wonderful items can be used to embellish your quilt: beads, threads, shells, charms, bells, tassels, sequins, ribbons, trims, lace, and buttons, just to name a few. The options are endless, and they are all such fun to collect! If you open your mind to the possibilities, you will be amazed at what you discover. Look at the photos that follow for some close-up details of embellishments on the quilts in this book.

Buttons are especially fun to collect. Novelty buttons come in many styles, themes, and colors. Buttons also make wonderful flower centers. You may sew the buttons on in the traditional manner, or you may tie them on so that the thread tails are on top of the button to act as the flower stamens.

To tie a button on, push the needle down through the buttonhole, leaving a 2" to 3" tail. Bring the needle back up through the opposite buttonhole and cut the thread 2" to 3" above the button. Tie the thread tails in a square knot to secure the button. Trim the threads so that they are ¼" to ½" long.

Button on "Divine Vines"

Embellishments on "Morning's Glory"

Netting with embellishments
used as overlay on "Tequila Sunrise"

Embellishments on "Falling Water"

Button cluster on "Peachy Keen"

ABOUT THE AUTHOR

Cynthia Tomaszewski operates her quilt-design company, Simple Pleasures (www. simpleas.com), from offices in Michigan and Abu Dhabi, United Arab Emirates, where she currently resides with her husband, Mike, and her Yorkie, Stanley. She and Mike plan to relocate one day to their idea of paradise, their acreage near Savusavu, on the island of Vanu Levu, Fiji. She is also the author of *Let's Pretend: Whimsical Quilts for Kids* (Martingale & Company, 2008). This is her fourth book.

Wearing flowers is an island tradition. Wearing a flower behind your right ear signifies your single status; wearing it behind your left ear means you've found the love of your life!

ACKNOWLEDGMENTS

Very special thanks to:

My husband, Mike, my problem solver and
dream companion. I'll love you always.

Donna Ward of Hamilton, New Zealand. Donna machine
quilted all the quilts in this book, except for "Tequila Sunrise."
Thank you for all of your beautiful work and that can-do
attitude that you carry with you always.

The staff of Martingale & Company,
the nicest team in the world to work with!
Your quality attitude and creative skills
make my quilts shine.

NEW AND BEST-SELLING TITLES FROM

APPLIQUÉ
Applique Quilt Revival
Beautiful Blooms
Cutting-Garden Quilts
Dream Landscapes
Easy Appliqué Blocks–NEW!
Simple Comforts–NEW!
Sunbonnet Sue and Scottie Too

BABIES AND CHILDREN
Baby's First Quilts
Baby Wraps
Let's Pretend
Snuggle-and-Learn Quilts for Kids
Sweet and Simple Baby Quilts

BEGINNER
Color for the Terrified Quilter
Happy Endings, Revised Edition
Machine Appliqué for the Terrified Quilter
Your First Quilt Book (or it should be!)

GENERAL QUILTMAKING
Adventures in Circles
American Jane's Quilts for All Seasons
Bits and Pieces
Bold and Beautiful–NEW!
Cool Girls Quilt
Country-Fresh Quilts
Creating Your Perfect Quilting Space
Fig Tree Quilts: Fresh Vintage Sewing– NEW!
Folk-Art Favorites–NEW!
Follow-the-Line Quilting Designs Volume Three
Gathered from the Garden
The New Handmade
Points of View
Prairie Children and Their Quilts
Quilt Revival
A Quilter's Diary, Written in Stitches
Quilter's Happy Hour
Quilting for Joy
Remembering Adelia–NEW!

Simple Seasons
Skinny Quilts and Table Runners
That Patchwork Place® Quilt Collection– NEW!
Twice Quilted
Young at Heart Quilts

HOLIDAY AND SEASONAL
Christmas Quilts from Hopscotch
Comfort and Joy
Holiday Wrappings

HOOKED RUGS, NEEDLE FELTING, AND PUNCHNEEDLE
Miniature Punchneedle Embroidery
Needle-Felting Magic
Needle Felting with Cotton and Wool

PAPER PIECING
Easy Reversible Vests, Revised Edition
Paper-Pieced Mini Quilts
Show Me How to Paper Piece
Showstopping Quilts to Foundation Piece
A Year of Paper Piecing

PIECING
501 Rotary-Cut Quilt Blocks
Favorite Traditional Quilts Made Easy
Loose Change
Maple Leaf Quilts
Mosaic Picture Quilts
New Cuts for New Quilts
Nine by Nine
On-Point Quilts
Quiltastic Curves
Ribbon Star Quilts
Rolling Along

QUICK QUILTS
40 Fabulous Quick-Cut Quilts
Instant Bargello
Quilts on the Double
Sew Fun, Sew Colorful Quilts
Supersize 'Em!–NEW!

SCRAP QUILTS
Nickel Quilts
Save the Scraps
Scrap-Basket Surprises–NEW!
Simple Strategies for Scrap Quilts
Spotlight on Scraps

CRAFTS
A to Z of Sewing–NEW!
Art from the Heart
The Beader's Handbook
Card Design
Crochet for Beaders
Dolly Mama Beads
Embellished Memories
Friendship Bracelets All Grown Up
Making Beautiful Jewelry
Paper It!
Trading Card Treasures

KNITTING & CROCHET
365 Crochet Stitches a Year
365 Knitting Stitches a Year
A to Z of Knitting
All about Knitting
Amigurumi World
Beyond Wool
Cable Confidence
Casual, Elegant Knits
Crocheted Pursenalities
Gigi Knits…and Purls
Kitty Knits
Knitted Finger Puppets
The Knitter's Book of Finishing Techniques
Knitting Circles around Socks
Knitting with Gigi
More Sensational Knitted Socks
Pursenalities
Simple Stitches–NEW!
Toe-Up Techniques for Hand-Knit Socks, Revised Edition
Together or Separate

Our books are available at bookstores and your favorite craft, fabric, and yarn retailers. If you don't see the title you're looking for, visit us at **www.martingale-pub.com** or contact us at:

1-800-426-3126

International: 1-425-483-3313
Fax: 1-425-486-7596 • **Email:** info@martingale-pub.com